13.56

W9-BND-237

all

DATE DUE			
OCT 3 1 1986			
AUG 1 2 1993			

Gaston Bachelard

Twayne's World Authors Series

Maxwell A. Smith, Editor of French Literature

Professor Emeritus, The University of Chattanooga

*Former Visiting Professor in Modern Languages,
The Florida State University*

TWAS 665

Illustration by Tamra Patton

Gaston Bachelard

By Roch C. Smith

The University of North Carolina at Greensboro

Twayne Publishers • Boston

Gaston Bachelard

Roch C. Smith

Copyright © 1982 by G. K. Hall & Company
All Rights Reserved
Published by Twayne Publishers
A Division of G. K. Hall & Company
70 Lincoln Street
Boston, Massachusetts 02111

Book production by Marne B. Sultz

Book design by Barbara Anderson

Printed on permanent/durable acid-free
paper and bound in The United States
of America.

Library of Congress Cataloging in Publication Data

Smith, Roch Charles, 1941–
   Gaston Bachelard.

   (Twayne's world authors series; TWAS 665)
   Bibliography: p. 153
   Includes index.
   1. Bachelard, Gaston, 1884–1962. I. Title.
II. Series.
B2430.B254S64   194   81–6089
ISBN 0–8057–6511–5   AACR2

To
Roch, Paul, and Mark

Contents

About the Author

A native of Sturgeon Falls, Ontario, Roch C. Smith is Professor of Romance Languages at the University of North Carolina at Greensboro, where he teaches courses in contemporary French literature. The recipient of an NDEA fellowship at Emory University, he holds the M.A. and Ph.D. in French from that institution as well as the B.A. and M.A.T. in Spanish from the University of Florida. His previous book, *Le Meurtrier et la vision tragique: Essai sur les romans d'André Malraux,* was published by Didier in 1975, and he has made a number of contributions on Malraux, Bachelard, and other figures to various learned journals, including *Symposium, French Literature Series, Science Technology and the Humanities, French Review, French Forum,* and *Comparative Literature Studies.* His translations of comtemporary French, Québécois, and Spanish-American poetry have appeared in several issues of *International Poetry Review,* and his annotated bibliography on Bachelard was included in the twentieth-century "Cabeen" bibliography of French literature. Dr. Smith has recently completed two articles: one on Malraux, for the *Studies in Twentieth Century Literature,* and the other on Bachelard, published in the *Stanford French Review.* He is currently engaged in a study of Samuel Beckett's novels.

Preface

Gaston Bachelard is one of the very few authors of our time who has dealt with the "two cultures," to borrow C. P. Snow's celebrated expression. Yet the English-reading public, usually more acquainted with Bachelard's works on the imagination than with his epistemology of science, tends to have a partial view of this versatile thinker. This can surely be attributed to the fact that only about one-fifth of his writings have been translated and that no book-length study in English examines both sides of his work. It is to fill the second lacuna that I have written this book, but always with the hope that it might stimulate some attention to the first.

I have also attempted to treat the related and very fundamental issue of the significance of Bachelard's epistemology of science for his theories of the imagination. While some critics have insisted that Bachelard's duality is irreconcilable, others have suggested that his works on the imagination owe something to his epistemology, although such suggestions have generally not been explored through a sustained analysis of that epistemology. During the six years I have spent studying Bachelard, however, an early suspicion has grown into a conviction that his philosophy of science must be understood in order truly to appreciate the full significance of his essays on the imagination and to assess properly his contribution to literary criticism.

Bachelard's books on science are not easy, and I am aware that my discussion of these texts may require some forbearance on the part of the general reader to whom this series is directed. But faced with the choice of a truncated and easily misleading presentation of Bachelard's thought, or an introduction to a fuller range of his work with a greater potential for reliability, I necessarily chose the latter. I have endeavored, however, to reduce the technical jargon to a minimum (not always an easy task with an author as fond of neologisms as Bachelard) and, with the exception of a single reference to the speed of light, I have managed to avoid altogether quoting passages with mathematical formulas. While I did keep some terms from science and philosophy, in many instances they could be expected to be understood more widely and in all cases they were clearer than any phrase that might have replaced them or they were key terms in Bachelard's own lexicon.

While Bachelard's work ultimately must be assessed from an established perspective, which in this case will be that of literature, he has such a formidable range of concerns that few can approach his work without venturing beyond the comfortable confines of a familiar discipline. Yet contemporary science and literature have taught Bachelard the value of transforming traditional modes of thought and established aesthetic canons—so readily maintained by specialists—into new possibilities, so that it is something of an advantage to approach him, at least in part, from the nonspecialist's unencumbered perspective.

I would not have completed such an undertaking, however, without the assistance of several colleagues, many of them experts in areas other than my own, who read portions of the manuscript and who endured with infinite patience my many attempts to clarify particular points. Professor Edouard Morot-Sir and Professor Robert B. Rosthal gave me valuable advice on dealing with Bachelard's epistemology. I am grateful to Professor Richard T. Whitlock for his insight and for his extremely lucid exposition of scientific issues. I wish also to thank Professor James C. Atkinson, who read the chapters on the imagination, and to express my particular gratitude to Professor William O. Goode, who graciously consented to read the entire manuscript, despite many obligations of his own. Any virtues this book may have are largely attributable to their efforts. Its faults are entirely my own. I extend my thanks also to Professor Maxwell A. Smith, who gave me excellent editorial advice while calmly bearing with my delays, to Professor E. Mary McAllester for her helpful comments on the final typescript, and to Professor Douglas W. Alden and Professor

Gerald Prince for their assistance in the early, bibliographical stages of this project.

For their translations of articles on Bachelard I thank Dr. Margo O. Bender (Italian), Mrs. Kathleen M. Bulgin (German), and Mrs. Margareta O. Thompson (Danish). Translations incorporated into the text are my own except in those cases where published translations of Bachelard's works exist. Initially, titles of published translations appear in the text after the French original. All other titles of Bachelard's works are translated in the Notes and References.

I gratefully acknowledge the support of the Research Council of the University of North Carolina at Greensboro in awarding me a research leave that allowed me to complete the writing and in funding portions of this project with several grants. I take particular delight in recognizing the contribution of two graduate students to this endeavor: Miss Sandra Corriher, who provided diligent bibliographical assistance when this project was still in its infancy, and Mrs. Betsy Simpson, who gave me the opportunity to direct her thesis on a Bachelardian reading of Camus's *La Chute*. I am most grateful to Mrs. Marie B. Bullard for her perseverance in obtaining materials on interlibrary loan. For her competent professionalism in typing an occasionally labyrinthine manuscript I thank Elizabeth Crabtree.

This effort would never have been sustained, or even begun, without the constant, often unspoken understanding and encouragement of my wife, Elaine, to whom I am deeply grateful. Her support and her active assistance in improving the manuscript and in proofreading the final draft were invaluable. Finally, to my sons for their interest and encouragement, and for their understanding and patience in the face of promises deferred, I dedicate this book.

Roch C. Smith

The University of North Carolina at Greensboro

Chronology

1884   Born June 27 in Bar-sur-Aube, in Champagne, of parents who are shopkeepers.

1895   Begins secondary studies at Bar-sur-Aube.

1902   Serves as teaching assistant (*répétiteur*) at the Collège de Sézanne.

1903   Postal clerk at Remiremont.

1906   Begins military service as a telegraphist in the Twelfth Dragoons at Pont-à-Mousson.

1907   Named postal agent at the Gare de L'Est station in Paris.

1909   Student of special mathematics at the Lycée Saint-Louis.

1912   Obtains a *licence* in mathematical science. Places third in the entrance examination for two openings at the École Supérieure de Télégraphie.

1913   On leave from the Post Office, he prepares for the examination for engineering students in telegraphy. Obtains a scholarship in mathematics from the Lycée Saint-Louis.

1914   July 8, marries a schoolteacher from his region. August 2, mobilized. Serves thirty-eight months in the trenches. Receives the Croix de Guerre.

1919   Begins teaching physics and chemistry at the Collège de Bar-sur-Aube.

1920   June 20, his wife dies and leaves him with a daughter, Suzanne. Obtains a *licence* in philosophy after one year of study.

1922   Obtains *agrégation* in philosophy. Teaches philosophy and science at Bar-sur-Aube.

1927 May 23, granted doctorate in letters at the Sorbonne. Theses directed by Abel Rey and Léon Brunschvicg. October 27, upon the invitation of Georges Davy, professor of philosophy, begins teaching two courses in philosophy every fortnight at the University of Dijon.

1928 *Essai sur la connaissance approchée* and *Étude sur l'évolution d'un problème de physique: La Propagation thermique dans les solides,* his two doctoral dissertations.

1929 *La Valeur inductive de la relativité.*

1930 Named to the chair of philosophy at the University of Dijon, where he develops a friendship with Gaston Roupnel.

1932 *Le Pluralisme cohérent de la chimie moderne* and *L'Intuition de l'instant.*

1933 *Les Intuitions atomistiques.*

1934 *Le Nouvel Esprit scientifique.*

1936 *La Dialectique de la durée.*

1937 Named *Chevalier* of the Legion of Honor. *L'Expérience de l'espace dans la physique contemporaine.*

1938 *La Formation de l'esprit scientifique* and *La Psychanalyse du feu.*

1939 *Lautréamont.*

1940 Named to the chair of history and philosophy of science at the Sorbonne, where he succeeds Abel Rey. Becomes the director of the Institute of the History of Science. *La Philosophie du non.*

1942 *L'Eau et les rêves.*

1943 *L'Air et les songes.*

1948 *La Terre et les rêveries de la volonté* and *La Terre et les rêveries du repos.*

1949 Returns to epistemology with the publication of *Le Rationalisme appliqué.*

1951 Promoted to the rank of *Officier* in the Legion of Honor. *L'Activité rationaliste de la physique contemporaine.*

1953   *Le Matérialisme rationnel.*

1954   Retires from the Sorbonne. Appointed Honorary Professor for an additional academic year (1954–55).

1955   Elected to the Academy of Moral and Political Sciences.

1957   *La Poétique de l'espace.*

1960   *La Poétique de la rêverie.* Elevated to rank of *Commandeur* in the Legion of Honor.

1961   Awarded the Grand Prix National des Lettres. *La Flamme d'une chandelle.*

1962   October 16, dies in Paris. Buried on October 19 at Bar-sur-Aube.

1970   Posthumous publication of *Le Droit de rêver* and of *Études.* July, Cerisy Colloquium on Bachelard.

1972   Posthumous publication of *L'Engagement rationaliste.*

Chapter One

The Man and His Times

The visitor entering the Sorbonne from number fifty-four Rue Saint Jacques soon comes upon one of that building's many amphitheaters or *amphis* as they are familiarly called: *l'amphi Gaston Bachelard*. This honor, which Bachelard shares with such personages as Descartes and Richelieu, commemorates the years from 1940 to 1955 when the professor with the provincial accent and the flowing beard would challenge his students to make philosophy take its lessons from science or to wonder with him at the surprising originality of a literary image. Standing before the students who had crowded into his small classroom on the second floor or who, with varying backgrounds in philosophy, had come to listen to one of his public lectures, Bachelard would find the most paradoxical example, the most unexpected figure to explain a difficult abstraction. Yet he would do so without sacrificing the concept to the illustration. It is a process he would often use in his writings on the philosophy of science. In both his teaching and his published works, whether dealing with science or the imagination, the undogmatic Bachelard would discard the superficial immediacy of the merely visual, in favor of a much deeper understanding of his subject. He had a rare talent for illustrating his lectures without diluting them, for charming his listeners into understanding his often difficult material, and for introducing those students too easily dazzled by abstractions to the wonders of an imagination inspired by matter. He was, as one student put it, "Gaston the magician."[1]

Not surprisingly, his colleagues at the university were not always comfortable with a "magician" occupying the chair of the history and philosophy of science. After all, virtually all his books before coming to the Sorbonne had dealt with the epistemology of science. They had included philosophical studies on the science of thermodynamics, on the theory of relativity, on chemistry and physics, as well as broader analyses of the "new scientific mind." It is true that with *La Psychanalyse du feu* [The Psychoanalysis of Fire] and *Lautréamont* he had revealed an interest in the imagination shortly before assuming his Sorbonne post, but those works had seemed an innocent aberration. Indeed, one of Bachelard's colleagues was convinced that there had been a misprint in the title of *La Psychanalyse du feu* and that it was really meant to be a much less disconcerting *Psychanalyse du fou*.[2]

Bachelard's subsequent publications on water, air, earth, and the dreaming imagination certainly did nothing to moderate the disquietude of some of his fellow scholars. Yet this new direction in his thought attracted its own followers and supporters, among them the poet Jean Lescure, with whom Bachelard shared a long friendship, and the engraver Albert Flocon, whose work Bachelard admired for its synthesis of the abstract and the concrete.[3] Besides, Bachelard's fellow philosophers of science were soon reassured by the publication, beginning in 1949, of three new epistemological essays in which he took up with renewed vigor and insight the particular relationship of rationalism and empiricism in modern science. Yet his work on the imagination was far from over. Following his retirement from the Sorbonne he guided his reader through reveries of space and candlelight in his three most poetic books. It was an apt conclusion to his life's work, for his was a lamp that burned with two flames, that of the rationalist and that of the dreamer. Once lit, both flames did not always burn with equal intensity, but neither one was ever fully extinguished.

The Intellectual Atmosphere

As an epistemologist, Bachelard was probably most influenced by the theories of the French philosopher of science, Léon Brunschvicg (1869–1944), who directed one of his two doctoral dissertations. From Brunschvicg Bachelard learned to respect the analytical rationality of discovery and to avoid the danger of relying on the didactic logic of prior synthesis. Such an approach was revolutionary at a time (the late 1920s and early 1930s) when many French epistemologists still followed the lead of Émile Meyerson, for whom identity, deduction, and a priori reason were fundamental principles in science. Brunschvicg also taught Bachelard to be receptive to the scientific revolution which took place, particularly in physics, during the first quarter of the twentieth century. Yet, as François Dagognet has shown, Bachelard was more willing than his mentor to enter into the fray and to consider specific problems of science in his epistemology.[4] It is from this willingness that stem some of his most original observations, particularly his notion that knowledge itself can become an obstacle to learning and that error can have a positive value in science.

Although Brunschvicg's influence was both direct and profound, the broader context of Bachelard's epistemological position includes the work of Henri Poincaré, whose emphasis on the importance of the imagination in formulating hypotheses Bachelard found particularly congenial, and Henri Bergson, about whom Bachelard was later to say that he accepted everything save continuity. Among earlier philosophers Bachelard owes much to Kant and, of course, to Descartes, against whom most Western philosophers, especially if they are French, seem compelled to define their thought. Bachelard, with his "non-Cartesian" epistemology, was certainly no exception.

Yet Bachelard was more than an epistemologist, and much of the transition from the rational to the realm of dreams, or the "oneiric," found its theoretical basis in Bergson, Freud, Jung, and other, lesser known figures, including Brazilian psychoanalyst Pinheiro dos Santos and French psychoanalytic critic Marie Bonaparte. But, as his work progressed, the impetus for this transition came less from theoreticians than from creative writers themselves. References to Poe, Novalis, Mallarmé, Valéry, Proust, and a host of surrealists and dadaists abound in his oneiric works. Bachelard's gargantuan appetite for literature, particularly poetry, was limited neither by established canons nor by national boundaries. The more his interest in the imagination grew, the more he relied on writers as his guides. His essays on the imagination are marked by progressively more intense attacks on positivistic literary criticism, whose rationalistic assumptions blind it to the originality and beauty of much contemporary literature. Bachelard is only occasionally specific about the targets of his complaints, but, given the critical context of the time, we can assume that these include the heirs of Taine, Faguet, Brunetière, and Lanson.[5]

An informed appraisal of Bachelard's contribution to literary criticism must be delayed until both his rationalistic and his oneiric works have been thoroughly discussed, but it should be made clear from the outset that, despite his growing interest in literature, his approach was primarily that of the philosopher interested in the imagination and, later, of the naive reader rejecting all scientific pretense. He rarely saw criticism itself as his task, so that there is little dialogue with contemporary critics whose positions might have been similar to his own. The reader will find an occasional mention of Albert Béguin, or of younger critics like Jean-Pierre Richard, but he is even more apt to encounter references to a favorite poet like Henri Bosco, Pierre-Jean Jouve, Jules Supervielle, or Rainer Maria Rilke. Bachelard is often seen as a founder of continental "new criticism," but, while he has affinities with Marcel Raymond, Georges Poulet, Jean Starobinski, Jean Rousset, and Roland Barthes, he belongs to no particular school. His scientific background and his tendency to reduce the literary text to its most striking images in order better to understand the workings of the imagination make him distinctive. His association of a "material" and a "dynamic" imagination with the four elements of antiquity make him unique.

Bachelard's Life

Gaston Bachelard was born on June 27, 1884, in Bar-sur-Aube, about two hundred kilometers southeast of Paris. The son of shopkeepers and the grandson of shoemakers, he grew up in the modest, earthy surroundings of this riverine town flanked by the low mountains and sloping vineyards of eastern Champagne. After completing his secondary schooling at Bar-sur-Aube, he spent a year as a teaching assistant in the nearby town of Sézanne before successfully applying for a position as a substitute clerk for the *Postes et Télégraphe* of Remiremont. There, despite an early ambition to become a newspaper editor, he developed an interest in telegraphy and, two years later, it was as a telegraphist that he enlisted for his tour of military service. Returning to the Post Office in 1907 he was assigned to the Gare de l'Est in Paris, where he was to remain until the eve of World War I.

With his sights now set on a career in engineering, Bachelard lost little time in taking advantage of the opportunities for additional training which Paris offered. For three years he took evening classes at the Lycée Saint Louis and in 1912, now twenty-eight years of age, he obtained his first diploma, a *licence* in mathematics. The same year he took an entrance examination for one of two openings in the *École supérieure de télégraphie* only to be refused admission when he placed third. Undeterred, he took a leave of absence from the Post Office, obtained a scholarship in mathematics from the Lycée Saint Louis, and prepared for the elimination examination offered to engineering students in telegraphy. But his life was soon interrupted by the outbreak of World War I. Married only three months, he was mobilized in 1914 and fought in the trenches for over three years.

Returning from the front with life, limb, and the Croix de Guerre, he gave up his plans to become an engineer and accepted a position teaching physics and chemistry in his old secondary school at Bar-sur-Aube. The following year, at age thirty-six, the recently widowed Bachelard took the first explicit step toward a new vocation when he successfully completed a *licence* in philosophy. Upon obtaining the *agrégation* two years later, he might have been expected to devote himself exclusively to teaching philosophy at Bar-sur-Aube, but, in an unusual step, he refused to abandon his science courses. Rather than changing his responsibilities, he merely increased them, working all the while on his two doctoral dissertations. His toil was rewarded when he obtained his doctorate at the Sorbonne in the spring of 1927. His two theses, an essay on knowledge by approximation, directed by Abel Rey, and a historical analysis of the problem of heat transfer in solids, under Brunschvicg's tutelage, were published the following year. At forty-four years of age Bachelard's career as a philosopher had now begun.

Although he continued to teach at Bar-sur-Aube for three more years, he was invited by Georges Davy, professor of philosophy at the University of Dijon, to teach two courses there every fortnight. During this period Bachelard pursued his interest in the philosophy of science, publishing *La Valeur inductive de la relativité* in 1929 and, the following year, accepting an appointment to the chair of philosophy at Dijon, where he was to remain for a decade. It was here that he established a close friendship with Gaston Roupnel, a physicist whose interests ranged far beyond his discipline.

In his 1927 book, *Siloë,* Roupnel, who was ultimately concerned with the relationship of reason and faith, developed a biological theory of time and habit. Following so closely on Bachelard's analysis of relativity, Roupnel's essay pointed to the possibility of a further exploration of time as a human experience. Moreover, Bachelard found a congenial colleague in this author of works on the French countryside for whom a special chair on the Burgundy dialect had been created at Dijon, and whose father was a modest railroad employee. Although he showed no signs of sharing Roupnel's concern with questions of faith, Bachelard became more adventuresome intellectually as a result of his encounter with this fellow provincial. In 1932, he published *L'Intuition de l'instant,* wherein he pondered some of the notions which Roupnel had advanced in *Siloë.* While many epistemological studies were still to follow, this signaled the first time that Bachelard had allowed himself to transcend the strict confines of his discipline. It would not be the last.

His years at the Sorbonne—where he occupied the chair of the history and philosophy of science from 1940 to 1954 and was named honorary professor for 1954–55—were particularly marked by the uniquely Bachelardian tension between science and poetry.[6] He would take pleasure in calling his students' attention to this duality by saying that he had the feet of a philosopher of science but the wings of a poet.[7] His writings, too, during this time reflected the science-poetry polarity with three works of epistemology and four on the imagination. And his appetite for reading in both areas was voracious. He literally "lost track of time" because of his reading when, as Albert Flocon reports, he removed the pendulum from his clock in order to make more room for books.[8]

But it was retirement in 1955 that gave Bachelard the greatest opportunity to chase the dreams which his reading inspired. The works of this period—*La Poétique de l'espace* [The Poetics of Space], *La Poétique de la rêverie* [The Poetics of Reverie], and *La Flamme d'une chandelle* [The Candleflame]—exhibit a surprising freedom from the taxonomic restraints that had guided his earlier essays on the imagination. The epistemologist, who some twenty years earlier had assumed the directorship of the Sorbonne's Institute of the History of Science, had now become a well-known and respected guide to the mysteries of the literary imagination, a status that was confirmed in 1961 when he was awarded the Grand Prix National des Lettres. The last major honor he was to receive (he had been elevated to the rank of *Commandeur* in the Legion of Honor the previous year and had been elected to the prestigious Academy of Moral and Political Sciences upon his retirement from the Sorbonne), it represented a national recognition of Bachelard's contribution to literary discourse. He died shortly thereafter, on October 16, 1962, and his body was returned to his native Bar-sur-Aube for burial.

Bachelard's Duality

Within a decade of Bachelard's death three posthumous collections of some of his previously published articles would attest to a continuing interest in both his scientific and poetic theories. In 1970 the philosopher Georges Canguilhem presented, under the title *Études,* five short essays which Bachelard had written between 1931 and 1934. Four of these essays show early signs of a broadening of Bachelard's epistemological concerns beyond the highly technical analyses of his early work to a more general consideration of the relationship of science and philosophy. But one essay in particular, "Le Monde comme caprice et miniature," stands out as an early discussion of the role of reverie in humanizing the world.[9] For Bachelard the epistemologist was already beginning to assert what he would later call his "right to dream." With the publication of *Le Droit de rêver* (1970) Philippe Garcin and *Les Presses Universitaires de France* applied Bachelard's declaration to an anthology of some twenty-six pieces dealing with the arts, literature, and reverie, all representative of the flowering of Bachelard's oneiric interests. In *L'Engagement rationaliste* (1972), its counterpart on the scientific side, Georges Canguilhem gathered thirteen articles showing Bachelard's "commitment to the rationality of reason, against its own tradition . . . against . . . the smug expression of a first success at rationalization."[10]

Clearly, Bachelard continues to have much to say both to those interested in epistemological questions and to students of the literary imagination. Will that continue? Or will one of the two aspects of his work eventually eclipse the other? The questions are speculative, of course, but they do lead to the related question of Bachelard's unity for which the text rather than an inscrutable future can be consulted. Some commentators conclude that Bachelard's obvious duality is just what it seems and is essentially irreconcilable, while others perceive hidden strands of unity within a tapestry that depicts the separation of science and poetry.[11] The issue may never be resolved in any satisfactory way, but, as the subsequent chapters will show, its consideration is unavoidable in any serious treatment of Bachelard. For it is a fact, unaccountable as it may be, that the author of an epistemological analysis of Einstein's theory of relativity and the writer of a poetic essay on candlelight are one and the same man.

Chapter Two

Early Epistemology

"To know," writes Bachelard at the beginning of his first book, "is to describe in order to retrieve."[1] A very great portion of his subsequent work elaborates this simple definition with its duality of description and recovery, of empirical observation and rational ordering. Like this opening sentence of his 1928 *Essai sur la connaissance approchée,* the entire monograph, which had been his major doctoral thesis, sets forth ideas and perceptions that are the seeds of much that is to follow in Bachelard's philosophy of science. Together with his secondary thesis on the problem of heat transfer in solids,[2] it sets the pattern for Bachelard's early work on the philosophy of science in which he illustrates his explorations of specific epistemological questions with problems drawn from a particular science.

The four books discussed in this chapter—*Essai sur la connaissance approchée, Étude sur l'évolution d'un problème de physique: La Propagation thermique dans les solides, La Valeur inductive de la relativité,* and *Le Pluralisme cohérent de la chimie moderne*—constitute a whole which, as Georges Canguilhem has pointed out, deals with the "distinctive traits of science at the beginning of the twentieth century—approximation, induction, coherence."[3] While Bachelard will eventually conclude that "man *has a destiny of knowledge,*"[4] his epistemological interests at this early stage are more narrowly focused, more specifically concerned with determining how knowledge takes place in science rather than, as will be the case later, with exploring the broader philosophical and even pedagogical consequences of that epistemology.

9

Knowledge by Approximation

Bachelard was less interested in developing a systematic theory of knowledge, as such, than in understanding and describing scientific thought.[5] His conclusions concerning the process of knowing reflect the experimental activity of modern science, especially as it seeks to understand microphenomena. For when science, particularly physics and chemistry, explores the world of the atom, it deals with a different order of experience, one that is outside the realm of everyday observation. As Bachelard repeatedly indicates throughout his epistemological works, this microphenomenal world may require systems of thought that, in some ways, contradict the logic of everyday experience. The study of microphenomena demands new methods not only because certain macrophysical laws do not apply but because the more detailed the scientist's measurement attempts to be, the more he discovers the inherent indeterminism of the structure of things.

This would seem paradoxical to a Newtonian physicist, for whom what is measured exists and is known in proportion to the precision of the measurement. According to this positivistic outlook, all other means of knowing give way to measurement, and this in turn guarantees the permanence of being. For the positivist, therefore, reality is what is measurable. But even in the macrophenomenal world, where Newtonian laws can still apply, the reduction of reality to measurement is problematic enough. For there is, Bachelard reminds us, a discrepancy between the exactness of mathematics, which can be viewed as absolute, and the necessary imperfection of any attempt at exactness when dealing with concrete reality. Our knowledge of reality can be made relatively precise, but never absolutely exact.

The problem is vastly compounded when the positivistic approach is applied to microphenomena. Here the eye never penetrates for it is the instrument that guides the scientist's search for knowledge. Aware that his measurement, refined as it may be, is necessarily inexact, the scientist attempts to limit errors since he cannot eliminate them completely. He recognizes that he is dealing with a different order of magnitude, one that requires different approaches in order successfully to yield knowledge. He must adapt his methods either to the first order of magnitude of everyday visual reality or to the second order of magnitude of microphenomenal reality as an initial step in limiting errors. "The order of magnitude thus becomes a first knowledge by approximation. . . . It is, in physics, the first act of thought by approximation" (*ECA*, 78). To know by approximation is to recognize the reality with which we are dealing and the ultimate inexactness of our means of measurement. And, although Bachelard maintains that knowledge of the first order of magnitude is also necessarily approximate, the notion of an approximation to reality is particularly relevant to microphenomenal knowledge.

Contemporary science has taught Bachelard the need to go beyond the knowledge of first approximation, to recognize that the scientist must abandon methods that worked in the macrophysical world. "The enemies of the scientist in the realm of second approximation are the scientific habits he has acquired while studying the first" (*ECA*, 70). The scientist who explores the world of second approximation must reject the notion of an admitted reality, for in the realm of second approximation nothing can be accepted as merely "given." Here the validity of what is known depends in large measure on mathematical precision. "If we want to know with maximum rigor, we must organize acts, totally substitute the *constructed* for the given" (*ECA*, 174, emphasis added). While Bachelard maintains that science eventually refers back to reality, it is his insistence on the new "constructive" role of mathematics that especially marks his epistemology.

Mathematics is not a science of objects but of abstract relations. As such it is nonempirical and what it constructs rationally can have a degree of arbitrariness with respect to empirical reality. Unlike the physics of first approximation that posits existence before knowledge, the constructive mathematics of second approximation proves the existence of a particular reality "only by comparison with other known elements or else by approximating them indefinitely" (*ECA*, 211). This indefinite approximation reflects the impossibility of ever applying absolutely exact measurement in a world where the "object" cannot otherwise be perceived. The scientist is literally at the mercy of his instruments and so must be extremely careful not to interject intuitions that belong to the more generally familiar macrophysical world. Indefinite approximation, for instance, does not presuppose, Bachelard reminds us, a fixed pole eventually to be reached by finer and finer approximations, one which would ultimately make approximation unnecessary. In the realm of second approximation, certainty is in the process, not in the never-to-be-attained goal.

Among the first-approximation notions that Bachelard feels compelled to transform in dealing with knowledge of second approximation is that of simplicity. It has long seemed axiomatic that the goal of science was to reduce or simplify reality in order to discover its hidden laws. In turn, such laws with their a priori simplicity were thought to guide the discovery of new details in a complex reality. Yet, if the value of a law lies in its simplicity but that law does not faithfully reflect microphysical reality, it does not meet the two tests of knowledge proposed by Bachelard: it does not adequately describe and therefore it cannot serve as a reference point for subsequent retrieval. Either simplicity is to be valued at the expense of adequate description or description is to be sought at the expense of simplicity. Bachelard escapes between the horns of the dilemma by proposing that simplicity be defined as clarity rather than reduction. Pointing out that the criteria of simplicity are relative to the scientific means at one's disposal, he suggests that "simplicity is not a state of things, but a veritable state of soul. We do not believe because it is simple, it is simple because we believe" (*ECA,* 101). Thus even ostensibly complex formulas are "simple" if they are believable, which, in this context, means if they are mathematically coherent, if they hold the "faith" of the rationalist.

The apparent paradox of defining rational complexity as simplicity is explained in Bachelard's second book, *Étude sur l'évolution d'un problème de physique: La Propagation thermique dans les solides* (1928), where he stresses that each solution to a problem clarifies the state of our knowledge. With the help of such clarifications, new mysteries are explored and a new clarity is acquired at the end of a complicated process, although an unforeseen fact may obfuscate erstwhile clear theories. In short, there is no intrinsic order of simplicity in the evolution of science. Rather than a search for hidden simplicity, or even for an intrinsic evolution from the simple to the complex, science is a rational conquest of complexity.

Using the history of the problem of heat transfer in solids as his illustration, Bachelard demonstrates that the clarity of present-day concepts of thermodynamics, or even seemingly "natural" notions such as temperature, is acquired through mathematical physics in which differential analyses ultimately converge to yield their own integral hypotheses. The acquired simplicity of these hypotheses is so secure that physicists no longer need to accept a coherent group of inductive, but prematurely simple generalizations merely because they have the practical advantage of providing immediate and accessible explanations. Thus "simplicity" for the physicist is what is mathematically clear, however complex it may be to the uninitiated. It has nothing to do with mere reduction.

Indeed, such reduction is a source of error that must be avoided by the scientist of second approximation. "We are less likely than before," Bachelard points out, "to find in the simplicity of a law proof of its truth, but from a pragmatic point of view, we prefer the less complicated of the laws which explain a phenomenon just as well" (*ECA*, 93). Less complicated here means the use of easier, more accessible mathematics. Such "intrinsic simplicity" (*ECA*, 94) may serve the practical purpose of explaining a particular phenomenon, but it may also complicate the effort to incorporate the phenomenon within a more general account and thus to establish its validity as knowledge.

Here again, the history of thermodynamics illustrates how a reductive, pragmatic simplicity can impede scientific progress. Before it occurred to anyone to use a fluid, such as mercury, to indicate the *effects* of heat, it was long imagined, Bachelard recalls that a real fluid, or "caloric," helped determine the *cause* of heat. Epistemologically, the problem with such an explanation is that it was content to deal with a specific phenomenon rather than to seek relationships between this phenomenon and others. "It is in vain that we would want to concentrate scientific thought on a separate object, and even on a phenomenon of determined order. Even more than common thought, scientific thought lives by relationships and it can know a phenomenon only by incorporating it into a system, or at least by bending it to the principles of a method" (*EEPP*, 157). What is learned on the basis of a single phenomenon does not permit discovery about a different phenomenon.

Such practical description is too closely bound to the object and generalizes too quickly. It lacks the degree of abstraction necessary to relate concepts one to another and thereby to expand knowledge, and as a hasty generalization it "retards discovery by giving facile confirmations to immediate hypotheses" (*EEPP*, 160). Mathematical abstraction, on the other hand, because it can be arbitrary with respect to observed reality, can incorporate all the pertinent possibilities of the phenomenon as it reconstructs it within the interconceptual framework of other discoveries. "In the study of thermal phenomena, the first sign of positivity is the break with all research on the nature of heat" (*EEPP*, 57). It is then that science learns to forego the inadequate explanation of immediate empiricism in favor of the rigors of abstraction.

This emphasis on the importance of abstraction is in counterpoise to Bachelard's insistence on physical reality as the ultimate test of knowledge. There is no contradiction here, for contemporary science has taught him that the old, a priori philosophical categories of empiricism and rationalism work dialectically in scientific practice. Dominique Lecourt, an informed critic of Bachelard's epistemology, has pointed out that, for Bachelard, the meaning of science is to be found in its own activity rather than in a "philosophical ideology" or "ideological philosophy."[6] Bachelard is not interested in making science fit a philosophical model but in adapting philosophy to an active, open-ended science. In doing so, he repeatedly stresses the dialectic of thought and matter, or, to put it in terms of his original definition of knowledge, of description and retrieval. No other pattern is more constant in Bachelard's entire epistemology.

In rejecting habits of first approximation, a priori simplicity, and immediate explanation, Bachelard emphasizes the preeminent role of epistemology. As he sees it, "truth seems . . . to refer solely to the procedures of knowledge. It cannot rise above the conditions of its verification" (*ECA,* 231). Any method, to be legitimate, "must be so, as a method, epistemologically. It has no call justifying itself by essentially ontological considerations" (*ECA,* 241). Contemporary science makes Bachelard highly skeptical of traditional ontology and its philosophical realism. Reality, for Bachelard, does not exist independently of the means of knowing. Thus traditional ontology must yield to a mathematically constructive rediscovery of reality. Such a "constructed realism" (*ECA,* 187) is perhaps best symbolized by the crystal, to which he returns in the conclusion of his *Étude sur l'évolution d'un problème de physique.*

The individual crystal repeats a pattern, with only slight variations, common to all crystals of the same substance, so that it may be seen both as a particular phenomenon and as a typical or generalized one. The patterns of the real crystal closely match those of an abstract, nonexistent crystal. "Between forms thus realized and ideal and abstract forms . . . , the correspondence is so narrow that we do not hesitate to see in them the trace of that intermediate realism that would doubtless be capable, if only we could extend it more, of bringing together mathematical and experimental laws" (*EEPP,* 173). The crystal symbolically unites not only the "descriptive," or empirical side of knowledge, but also its "retrieval," or rational side.

On the one hand is the phenomenon being studied; on the other is a constructive mathematics that goes beyond quantitative description and projects possibilities through an inductive process of synthesis. The success of such mathematics, not only as mathematics but also as physics, is assured both by its rational coherence and by an eventual accord with experimental reality. Such an accord is made possible by a "creative intuition [which] remains the choice intermediary between logic and experiment" (*EEPP,* 170). The source of this union is necessarily intuitive for Bachelard because the coherence of constructive mathematics is self-sufficient—there is no *logical* necessity for it to lead back to reality. Thus any ontological prejudices must be abandoned in favor of an intuitive, constructive method that "rediscovers" reality mathematically.

Induction—*La Valeur inductive de la relativité*

In 1919 Einstein's theory of general relativity was experimentally validated when British astronomers were able to confirm certain predictions of his theory by measuring the gravitational deflection of starlight during a solar eclipse. While this event made Einstein "an almost god-like figure in the public eye,"[7] as one biographer put it, his stature among his peers was already well established on the basis of his revolutionary theories. It would seem perfectly appropriate, therefore, that a philosopher of science such as Bachelard should not only include a discussion of Einstein's special and general relativity in his epistemological studies but also devote an entire book to a consideration of theories that so fundamentally transformed contemporary science. In *La Valeur inductive de la relativité* (1929) Bachelard attempts to place the theory of relativity in the context of the history of science and to assess its revolutionary role both for physics and for mathematics. In so doing, he pursues his own preoccupation with a dialectically empirical and rational knowledge. Yet, in this case, he stresses the rational side of the equation to the virtual exclusion of the empirical aspect. He seems to have found in Einstein a congenial rationalist, or at least that is the aspect of Einstein's thought that most appeals to Bachelard.

Taking as his point of departure the newness of relativity theory, its "dialectical" break with Newtonian doctrines, he begins by showing that, despite some attempts to see in Einstein's theory a continuation of Newton's system through quantitative rediscovery, "the two systems, Newtonian and Einsteinian, appear to have no resemblance, no link, no inductive kinship."[8] The break between the two methods is "irrevocable," their systems of thought are "entirely heterogeneous" (*VIR,* 44), Bachelard insists. "Relativity does not *continue* former doctrines, it *rectifies* them" (*VIR,* 184). And while he recognizes that Newtonian physics continues to have a practical application, Bachelard warns of the danger for epistemology of accepting what is now only a pragmatic solution as a general and valid method of knowing reality.

In dealing with the newness of Einsteinian theories, Bachelard's central preoccupation is with the revolutionary role of mathematics, which he had previously identified as the hallmark of contemporary science. He points out that in Einsteinian physics the mathematics of discovery does not proceed deductively from certain quantified laws based on prior observation and experiment. Rather, the calculus of relativity initially generalizes in order to account for all variables. It is synthetic, or inductive, rather than analytic, or deductive, in its initial approach. Mathematics is not used merely to describe reality in quantitative terms; through its constructive processes, it has become a means of discovering reality. "We are thus led to oppose to the simplifying role of mathematical information, the constructive role of mathematical induction" (*VIR*, 84–85). It is not merely a question of physics having become more mathematical, "it is to the very center of physics that mathematics has just gained access and it is now the mathematical impulse that gives to the progress of physical science its force and its direction" (*VIR*, 83–84). Inductive mathematics has become the tool of discovery for the new physics.

From a philosophical perspective, the striking value of an inductive mathematics that sets out to account for all the variables is that it incorporates possibility into a rational system: "In the doctrines of relativity more than in any other, the affirmation of a possibility appears as an antecedent to the affirmation of a reality; the possible is then the a priori framework of the real. And it is calculus that places the real in its true perspective, at the heart of a coordinated possibility. The mind then accepts a reality that has become a piece of its own game" (*VIR*, 81). The inductive mathematics of relativity aims at establishing, through differential calculus, "the map of the possible" (*VIR*, 140). It is guided, not by what is realizable within existing experimental constraints, but by what can be conceived within much broader rational constraints, "what it is possible to imagine and coordinate with other possible experiments" (*VIR,* 143–44). Here imagination and intuition no longer merely bridge the gap between a rational system and reality. Because inductive mathematics incorporates possibility, the imagination has an important collateral role to play within the rational system itself.

Indeed, in relativity, where "one sees only because one foresees" (*VIR,* 52), the epistemological relationship of reason and reality has been reversed, so that instead of being *followed* by retrieval, description is now *preceded* by prediction. The delicate balance between empiricism and rationalism is preserved in Bachelard's epistemology, but, following the lessons of relativity, the initial emphasis is given to the rationalistic side of the equation. For it is the formal, mathematical aspect of relativity which, for Bachelard, revolutionizes physics. Here, after all, is a theory in which the speed of light is formalized into a postulate, so that "it is the sign c rather than the number 3×10^{10} centimeters [per second] that counts" (*VIR,* 148). In Bachelard's view, the *empirical* value of the speed of light is secondary in relativity; it has become a fundamental speed that serves as a reference for other relations.

Here, then, is a theory that initially stands on its own internal coherence rather than on its reference to empirical evidence. In fact, experimentation has followed this mathematically inductive theory with some delay. Bachelard sees in these delays "one of the most decisive proofs of the formal character of relativist construction" (*VIR,* 154). It is a synthetic method which constructs before it describes, one for which mathematical invention precedes reality. Thus, it is not surprising that at least one commentator suspects that Bachelard, despite his frequent protestations to the contrary, latently adheres to an a priori rationalistic tradition.[9] Such a view is surely extreme when the entire body of Bachelard's epistemology is taken into account, although it is somewhat more understandable when one considers his treatment of relativity in particular.

Aside from the decidedly preeminent role of reason, the philosophical conclusions to be drawn from Bachelard's consideration of relativity are not appreciably different from those of his two earlier studies. Here, as before, *traditional* ontological perspectives have no philosophical bearing. The attributes of a phenomenon are not related to its "substance" but are a function of mathematical relation. "The attribute without relation," quips Bachelard, "is a check with insufficient funds" (*VIR,* 209). For any talk of "being" to still have meaning in such circumstances, it must be recognized that mathematical relation is fundamental: "By pushing relativity to what we believe to be its metaphysical consequences, in this way, we have the impression that the mathematical conditions that serve as its point of departure are multiplied and extended in an ontology that is all the more coherent for being of mathematical essence" (*VIR,* 211). As was the case in his two earlier studies, such an "ontology" cannot be confused with the traditional ontology of philosophical realism with its emphasis on substance rather than relation. We see, once again, that the real does not exist independently of our method of knowing for Bachelard. Indeed, in the case of relativity, he even takes a further step in the direction of a preeminent rationalism. When he points out that relativity "organizes entities before posing . . . the essentially secondary problem of their reality" (*VIR,* 213), he seems to be saying that the real does not *pre*exist our method of knowing it.

In suggesting a conclusion that is so extreme and paradoxical (at least from the standpoint of realism), Bachelard is well aware that he is going beyond Einstein's own position. "Einstein seems to adopt the traditionally realist point of view in that he supposes that matter is in a sense anterior to space" (*VIR,* 219). Bachelard's view on the philosophical consequences of Einstein's theory, particularly that of general relativity, is inspired instead by those of Sir Arthur Stanley Eddington, one of the British astronomers who confirmed that theory during the solar eclipse of 1919. While it would be beyond the scope of this book to explore at length Eddington's epistemology, it is illuminating nonetheless to take into account certain striking similarities with Bachelard's position.

Eddington, like Bachelard, stresses the dichotomy between common sense, three-dimensional realism from which science began and the four-dimensional world of relativity that replaces it: "the real three-dimensional world is obsolete and must be replaced by four-dimensional space-time with non-Euclidian properties."[10] But, again like Bachelard, and unlike Einstein, Eddington is not prepared to assume the antecedence of matter. He is struck, instead, by the formal character of relativity, by its structural properties: "The theory of relativity . . . is knowledge of structural form, and not knowledge of content. All through the physical world runs that unknown content, which must surely be the stuff of our consciousness. . . . Where science has progressed the farthest, the mind has but regained from nature that which the mind has put into nature."[11] For Eddington, the rational patterns of the mind determine what we know of reality.

Bachelard's view of reality as secondary to its organization is consistent with Eddington's supposition that "the investigation of the external world is a quest for *structure* rather than substance."[12] In taking note of Eddington's particular emphasis on the structural aspect of scientific knowledge, the reader of Bachelard can appreciate a similar point of view in the latter's epistemology. While Bachelard does not insist, as does Eddington, on the term "structural" or "structure," the proximity of both philosophers' views and Bachelard's frequent insistence on the "constructive" or "reconstructive" role of mathematics make it apparent that he too was thoroughly familiar with the structural aspect of modern science.

Coherence—*Le Pluralisme cohérent de la chimie moderne*

Having explored the rationalistic dimension of knowledge in the congenial realm of relativity theory, Bachelard then undertakes, in *Le Pluralisme cohérent de la chimie moderne* (1932), the challenge of demonstrating the fundamental rationalism of that seemingly less kindred domain, the "supremely experimental and positive science"[13] of chemistry. His stated goal is to examine the dialectic oscillation in chemistry between the diversity of heterogeneous elements, or "pluralism, on the one hand, and the reduction of plurality, on the other" (*PCCM,* 5). Since much of this fluctuation takes place over time, his approach is necessarily partly historical, although he disclaims any intent to write a history of chemistry, as such.[14] As was the case previously, knowledge is conceived in terms of a binary opposition—in this case, of pluralism and coherence—although it would be a distortion, as Bachelard shows, ultimately to assume a facile association of empiricism and rationalism with either pluralism or coherence. Such an association may well be justified historically, but he is able to demonstrate the eventual interplay of both pairs of oppositions in modern chemistry.

While Bachelard emphasizes that any unifying thought in science must facilitate a new diversity, he claims that, in the abstract, it does not really matter if knowledge begins with the perception of diversity or the constitution of identity since knowledge stops neither in diversity nor in identity. Yet, because the prescientific era and even the early scientific age[15] assumed not only a naive realism but a universal natural order or *"naive harmony"* which was impatient with "the delays and precautions of empiricism" (*PCCM,* 225), modern chemistry had to begin not with unity but with diversity. Thus, chemistry originally multiplied the number of substances. In doing so, it reinforced naive realism while it abandoned an assumed unconstructed harmony.

In a series of chapters, Bachelard shows that the chemist began by looking for individual qualities of substances but ended by finding general laws as the initial, surface realism of experimental chemistry opened the way to the rationalism of mathematical chemistry. Contemporary chemistry, Bachelard points out, is suspicious of immediate sensation. It goes beyond the immediate quality to a hidden one which is relative because it appears as the result of a relationship of bodies. Accessible bodies in a chemical phenomenon are primarily of interest as pieces of a construction. "It is therefore on a deep plane that chemical analysis must find its root" (*PCCM,* 39). In contemporary chemistry, depth of rational construction replaces surface description.

Recounting the efforts, principally of Mendeleev, to fix the order of elements according to atomic weight, Bachelard gives particular emphasis to the subsequent shift from atomic weight to atomic number as a classificatory principle. Unlike the atomic weight, the atomic number did not initially correspond to empirical observation; it was merely the ordinal number of a particular element in Mendeleev's chart. Yet this apparently artificial variable, which originally had no experimental meaning, gradually took on increasing value as an experimental tool and point of reference. For Bachelard, this was "one of the greatest theoretical conquests of the century" (*PCCM*, 134). It meant that a particular substance could be known by its place on the periodic chart even before it was empirically "discovered" or "produced." It is hardly surprising that Bachelard should underscore this particular aspect of chemistry, for it is difficult to imagine a more immediate and vivid example of the rationalism of discovery.

Bachelard's examination of the chemistry of second approximation, that of the chemical atom, or what he calls "electrical chemistry," further reinforces his thesis that in chemistry, too, the balance needs to be struck in the direction of rationalism. "Beneath the interplay of multiple and mixed qualities which constitute our immediate phenomenon and which the phenomenon of ordinary chemistry still reaches, a profound quality is disclosed in the experiments of electrical chemistry. This quality turns out to be totally uniform, it is suitable for constituting an essentially instrumental and schematic phenomenon that is eminently accessible to reason" (*PCCM*, 167). As chemistry becomes more theoretical and mathematical, as it moves away from a first approximation study of substance, the variety of the elements is gradually replaced by the uniformity of electrons. As it becomes increasingly rational and ordered, chemistry turns away from the naive realism of its beginnings. Having relinquished an assumed harmony in favor of realism, chemistry now has made a paradoxical reconversion to harmony. Yet the paradox is only apparent, for the real transformation is not from harmony to realism and back again, but from a naive view of harmony and reality to a rationally constructed view of each. For, despite its rational aspect, chemistry does not really abandon reality; it ultimately deals with chemical elements, even if the qualities of such elements are now considered secondary to the uniform qualities of the chemical atom.

In becoming more rational, chemistry demonstrates "how diversity can be born of identical components" (*PCCM*, 169) by constructing well-ordered variations from the uniform qualities of the chemical atom. In chemistry, what is systematically possible can be, and often is, brought into being. It becomes an empirically inventive, constructive science that actively combines the pluralism of diversity with the coherence of ordered harmony. "Chemical substances, included in a coherent and harmonic pluralism, suggest possibilities of construction" (*PCCM*, 228). The dialectical oscillation between pluralism and coherence that took place sequentially in the history of chemistry has been transformed through rationalism into the very means of knowing in modern chemistry. An equally dialectical but synchronic "coherent pluralism" has replaced diachronic oscillation as modern chemistry has grown more rational.

While Bachelard never abandons the empirical or "descriptive" side of the knowledge equation, it is quite evident that the "retrieval" or, increasingly, the "constructive" side is given significant attention. Contemporary science is always experimental, of course, but in Bachelard's early epistemology and beyond, it is its rational aspect that makes it distinctive. In Bachelard's view, contemporary science teaches us the need not so much to *see* better, but to think more accurately.

Chapter Three
The New Scientific Mind

The year 1932 marks a broadening of Bachelard's interests to include not only epistemology but some attempts at metaphysics. Despite this shift, the underlying perspective of *L'Intuition de l'instant* (1932) and of *Les Intuitions atomistiques* (1933) remains that of the philosopher of science. While these two books provide the first clues to what will eventually develop into Bachelard's "oneiric," as opposed to his "rationalist," side, at this stage oneiric preoccupations are still secondary to his continued interest in epistemology. During the period from 1934 to 1940, however, his concerns within epistemological works themselves, such as, *Le Nouvel Esprit scientifique* and, especially, *La Formation de l'esprit scientifique,* gradually widen. Bachelard now demonstrates a growing preoccupation with what he regards as the danger of imagistic thinking for science, and with questions of the pedagogical consequences of science.

His main interest is still epistemology, but the epistemological essays of this period are generally less technical and more accessible to the reader uninitiated to science. In contrast to his earlier epistemological writings, for example, only one work of this period, *L'Expérience de l'espace dans la physique contemporaine,* concentrates on the philosophical significance of particular questions in a specific science. In the seven years from *Le Nouvel Esprit scientifique* to *La Philosophie du non,* Bachelard is especially concerned with clarifying and summarizing the revolutionary character of those philosophical attributes which have grown out of scientific activity. It is this revolutionary contribution of science to philosophy that allows him to speak of a "new scientific mind."

A Transcendent Science

In attempting to bring out the revolutionary aspect of science, Bachelard returns in *Le Nouvel Esprit scientifique* (1934) to several features of contemporary science which he had treated more extensively in his earlier work. References to the inductive and synthetic qualities of mathematical science are already familiar to the informed Bachelard reader. The notion that entities are uniform within an atomic group or that what is simple is what is clarified mathematically had been explored previously as well. If Bachelard comes back to these observations, it is undoubtedly to make his point about the newness of science more effectively and, perhaps, to widen his audience. For the freshness of this book lies less in the detailed points it makes than in its comprehensive emphasis on the nature of contemporary science.

Bachelard's point of departure is remarkably similar to that of his *Essai sur la connaissance approchée,* namely the active association of rationalism and empiricism in modern science. But, where this association served to define knowledge in his first book, its purpose here is more broadly philosophical, for it is used to resist the doctrinaire imposition of absolute, a priori philosophical categories on an active science. "Science, in fact, creates philosophy"[1] and this new philosophy must abandon the strictures of preconceived ideas; it must be prepared to modify traditional philosophical vocabulary as it adapts to the flexibility and mobility of science.

Among the a priori views that need to be transformed is the notion that knowledge generalizes our perception of reality. Scientific realism, contrary to traditional, positivistic, and pragmatic views, is a hybrid of rationalism and empiricism in which the "epistemological *vector* seems very clear. It surely goes from the rational to the real and not the reverse—from reality to the general" (*NES,* 4). An inductive reason finds its confirmation in scientific experiment, in the reality it reconstructs, while *immediate* reality is merely a pretext for scientific thought and not an object to be known. "The teachings of reality are worthwhile only to the extent that they suggest rational realizations" (*NES,* 9). Meaningful reality in contemporary science, Bachelard insists, is the result of rational projects, so that the role of observation is primarily to follow and confirm an essentially rational experiment. Observation "reconstructs the real after having reconstructed its diagrams" (*NES*, 12). Science invents its own objects, it constructs its own world, subject only to eventual confirmation of its constructs by experimentation.

Bachelard suggests that, in contemporary science, where a "phenomenotechnique . . . learns by what it constructs" (*NES*, 13), scientific observation "transcends the immediate" (*NES*, 12). It is a transcendent science in the sense that it goes beyond not only immediate reality, but earlier systems of science and mathematics by restructuring them on a new basis rather than by denying their validity altogether. Just as common reality is transformed by science, so is the geometry of Euclid transformed by subsequent geometries, the mechanics of Newton by subsequent physics, and, ultimately, the epistemology of Descartes by subsequent epistemology.

Non-Euclidian Geometry

Reviewing the history of geometry during the nineteenth century, Bachelard recognizes the rough outlines of a Hegelian dialectical pattern when mathematicians like Taurinus, Bolyai, and Lobachevsky challenge Euclid's fifth postulate on parallel lines and propose an alternate geometry.[2] This "antithesis" to Euclid's "thesis" is resolved, according to Bachelard, into the "synthesis" of an axiomatic, generalized geometry in which "Euclidian geometry will be found in its place within a whole, as a particular case" (*NES*, 27). In the dialectical history of geometry, the thesis is not denied; it conserves its form, if not its original influence, when it is incorporated into a synthetic general geometry. Where, in earlier mathematics, parallels were thought to reflect physical reality, it is now understood that geometric elements are "relational and not at all substantial" (*NES*, 29), that they stem from reason and not from reality. As in science, reality follows the formal constructs of geometry, especially as the various geometries are made to correspond to each other through the transformation of their elements. "It is by making geometries correspond that mathematical thought takes on reality. In this way, a mathematical form is known by its transformations. One could say to a mathematical being: tell me how you are transformed, I will tell you who you are" (*NES*, 28).

Reality is not to be found in any one postulate, which, by itself, is arbitrary. Rather it is in the synthetic correspondence of these various postulates that mathematics makes the link with reality possible. When mathematical relations form a coherent body, a totality, that cohesion of thought is ready to correspond to objective reality. As Bachelard indicates, "it is then that geometric thought gives the impression of a totality and it is then only that the coherence of thought seems to be matched by an objective cohesion" (*NES*, 30). Bachelard compares the relations of separate geometric forms to syllables made up of separate letters. Just as syllables have no meaning until they are combined to form a word, so mathematical forms and relations can have no objective meaning until they are coordinated. This symbolic reduction of mathematics to a kind of morphology indicates "the poetic effort of mathematics, the creative, effectuating effort" (*NES*, 31). Like language, in which meaning is achieved through the association of discrete elements, mathematics has a semantic quality, since here, too, meaning is not to be found in the separate forms but in their association into a totality: "This sudden semantic value [of mathematics] is essentially totalitarian; it appears in the completed sentence, not in the root. Thus, at the moment the notion is presented as a totality, it plays the role of a reality" (*NES*, 31).

We have noted previously that Bachelard's epistemology brings out the "constructive" or "reconstructive" attributes of contemporary science and that science is opposed to a phenomenology of objects perceived as "givens" by a subject. The terms "constructive" or "reconstructive" and the concept of a rationally coordinated science which such terms represent indicate Bachelard's view of science as a structuralist activity.[3] Moreover, it is precisely the structural aspect of modern mathematics that Bachelard emphasizes in *Le Nouvel Esprit scientifique*. As Jean Piaget points out, "in mathematics, structuralism is opposed to the compartmentalization of heterogeneous subjects by recovering unity thanks to isomorphisms."[4] Bachelard's emphasis on transformation, totality, and internal coherence in mathematics is echoed in Piaget's observation that a structure, whether in mathematics or elsewhere, includes "the three characteristics of totality, transformation, and self-regulation."[5]

Thus, in developing a philosophy that takes its lessons from science, Bachelard "discovers" structuralism before the term falls into more general use and before the concept is applied more widely. That he should call attention to the "semantic" attribute of mathematics in the context of his discussion of their structural activity, suggests that Bachelard may well have had an incipient sense of the more general applicability of the structuralism of science and mathematics. In any case, he is clearly well acquainted with the concepts of structuralism despite the fact that he does not use the term.

Non-Newtonian Physics

Somewhat later, but perhaps more dramatically than was the case with the development of non-Euclidian geometry, Albert Einstein projected physics beyond the orthodoxies of mechanical physics, whose origins were to be found in Newton. Bachelard examines anew the relationship of Newtonian and Einsteinian thought, but unlike his earlier treatment of this question in *La Valeur inductive de la relativité,* his analysis now explicitly avoids the use of mathematical equations, a fact that undoubtedly contributes to making *Le Nouvel Esprit scientifique* a more accessible and consequently a better-known work.

Bachelard gives renewed emphasis to the fact that there is no real transition from Newton to Einstein. Einstein's theories represent a radical departure from Newtonian physics, a restructuring of the very foundations of physics. "One follows, therefore, a transcendent induction and not an amplifying induction in going from classical to relativist thought" (*NES,* 42). Yet, once the theory of relativity is established as the basis for physics, it is possible, through a process of reduction, to obtain classical Newtonian thought. In transcending Newtonian physics, therefore, Einstein's theory does not deny it, but reconstructs it and incorporates it into a new, non-Newtonian physics, in much the same way that Lobachevsky's geometry restructured and encompassed that of Euclid. Where Lobachevsky's geometry challenged Euclid's postulate on parallels, Einstein's relativity challenges the ideas of simultaneity, which seemed so basic in classical physics. With Einstein, Bachelard reminds us, the measurement of time and space is not absolute but relative to the means of measuring. This challenge to absolute time and space is soon followed by Heisenberg's uncertainty principle, which describes how a precise experiment with infinitely small phenomena necessarily affects those phenomena so that the experiment itself becomes part of the reality being explored.

While Bachelard will not examine fully the ontological implications of these challenges to the classical Newtonian view of reality until after he has published his works on the imagination of fire, water, air, and earth, he does recall, once again, that in contemporary science, mathematical rationalism reconstructs reality. In allying the possible with the real through constructs which precede objective reality, the activity of science, like that of mathematics, resembles that of poetry. "In remembering those beautiful mathematical symbols where the possible and the real are allied, can we not evoke Mallarméan images?" (*NES,* 56) asks Bachelard. Ultimately, mathematical physics must deal, not with absolutes, but with experimental possibilities. "Reality is rediscovered as a particular case of the possible" (*NES,* 58). As is true with much contemporary poetry, beginning with late-nineteenth-century symbolism, contemporary science is projective rather than descriptive.[6]

Once his work on the imagination is under way, Bachelard will emphasize the differences between science and poetry. But it is noteworthy that, before he has any reason to fear leading his reader astray because of the dual nature of his writings, and before he defines science in opposition to an imagination born of naive realism, he feels free to hint at a parallel between science and poetry and to suggest that a kind of mathematical creativity, similar to the imaginative and linguistic creativity of the poet, is an essential aspect of scientific activity.[7] Both science and poetry create a "presence" of possibilities, the one mathematically conceived, the other verbally imagined, before any link to physical reality is established. As Bachelard sees it, both science and poetry can be said to project a particular reality rather than merely to reflect it.

Bachelard examines this projective quality of science in light of the matter-radiation, wave-particle, determinism-indeterminism contrasts of contemporary science. Here an "ontological dialectic" in which "description is replaced by equation" (NES, 65) challenges traditional philosophical realism whose topological language reflects the implicit assumption that reality is made up of objects located in time and space. The constructed phenomena of science, such as electron spin, have no meaning in isolation. One may *imagine* the spin of an isolated electron, for example, but one does not *think* it. Thinking, in the science of second approximation, depends on mathematical relations. Without these relations the phenomena of science cannot meaningfully be said to exist. In contemporary science "objects have a reality only in their relations" (NES, 132). All else is imagination.

This primacy of relation not only destroys former absolutes such as time, space, matter, and motion but makes problematic the traditional notions of cause and effect. The association of waves and particles in microphysics, for example, is not causal. Taken separately, they are mere images, not objects that can have an effect on other objects in the manner of the traditional mechanical model of physics. "The particle and the wave are not things that are linked by mechanisms. Their association is of a mathematical order; they must be understood as different moments of the mathematization of the experiment" (NES, 95). In Bachelard's view it is more accurate to speak of probabilities rather than a mechanistic law of cause and effect. The statistical laws of chance govern the phenomena of second approximation and, as is the case with other aspects of contemporary science, contradict traditional realism. Rather than the determinism of universal cause and effect, science teaches that there can be a convergence of probabilities, that the cause and effect relationship is probabilistic rather than deterministic. The phenomena of science are group phenomena, governed by the statistical laws of groups. They are not simple entities isolated by analysis, but complex elements constructed by synthesis.

Non-Cartesian Epistemology

The new science brings about a "difficult epistemological reversal" (*NES,* 139) since it discovers reality by means of inductive synthesis rather than by Cartesian reductive analysis. Where Descartes proposed a method of reducing phenomena to their simplest elements in order to understand them, contemporary science embarks upon a process of discovery through mathematical extension or construction in which all possible variables are taken into account. Such an approach may eventually lead back to the Cartesian goal of simplicity, but only after all the relations have been incorporated into the theoretical or experimental phenomenon. In contemporary science, as Bachelard has indicated earlier, simplicity comes at the end of mathematical construction—it follows an initial complication, it is a result.

The new science, therefore, is not opposed to Cartesian goals but to Cartesian methods. It is not anti-Cartesian but non-Cartesian in the sense that it goes beyond Cartesianism by widening its basis and ultimately incorporating it. Yet one of the most astute observations of *Le Nouvel Esprit scientifique* is that this shift in method, this epistemological reversal, has necessary consequences for our notion of reality. Bachelard summarizes his position by paraphrasing, once again, a well-known French proverb: " 'Tell me how you are sought, I will tell you who you are' " (*NES,* 139).[8] The point is clear: how we know determines what we know. Without denying their necessary link, Bachelard considers epistemology rather than ontology to be a more fundamental consequence of science.

As Bachelard sees it, Cartesian ontology involves the necessary participation of the subject. In examining an immediate reality of substance, such as a piece of wax, the Cartesian observer changes as that reality changes: "If the wax changes, I change" (*NES,*

168), claims Bachelard. In order to reflect the desired elimination of this subjective substantialism in contemporary science, Bachelard proposes that Descartes's famous *cogito ergo sum* be modified to a passive *cogitatur ergo est* ("it is thought, therefore it is"). Such a formula would more accurately render the primacy of method so central to Bachelard's view of science. It would be in keeping with his emphasis on the rational, constructive objectivity of the new science since what "is" is not affirmed as the product of universal consciousness or reason, as in Descartes's "I am," but is the limited consequence of a specific process of thought.

Rather than a Cartesian discourse on the method of knowing reason well, Bachelard proposes, as one critic suggests, a "Discourse on the method of constructing reason well. . . ."[9] Such a constructive activity cannot take place in the presence of preexisting orthodoxies. It is not a question of knowing how reason operates universally, based on outmoded concepts of reality, but of learning what the activity of contemporary science has to teach about the rational process as it discovers new realities. Science is a correction of past errors, a broadening of knowledge and of the rational process which "judges its historical past by condemning it" (*NES,* 173). It progresses by casting doubt on past certainties. And so, paradoxically, science maintains an open doubt on its past, a sort of Cartesian universal doubt. Yet, as Bachelard himself points out, "here again is an attitude which goes beyond, prolongs, and amplifies Cartesian prudence and which deserves to be called non-Cartesian, always in the same sense that non-Cartesianism is a completed Cartesianism" (*NES,* 165). The new scientific mind rectifies; it does not destroy.

The Experience of Space

The chief concern of *L'Expérience de l'espace dans la physique contemporaine* (1937) is to demonstrate how the proposals previously put forward in *Le Nouvel Esprit scientifique* can be supported by a more narrowly defined and more technical analysis of physics. Yet, despite its more technical nature and the similarities of its conclusions with those of the earlier work, *L'Expérience de l'espace* is of particular interest because it deals with space as an experience and, as such, will have its imaginative counterpart some twenty-three years later in *The Poetics of Space*. This is not to suggest that the word "experience" can, in any sense, have the same meaning in both contexts. On the contrary, the experience of space that will be explored in *The Poetics of Space* is subjective while the experience of space in contemporary physics is exclusively a rational construct. Here the ambiguity of the French word *expérience* comes into play as what was once an "experience" is increasingly identified with "experiment." In microphysics space is obviously not experienced, as it might be in a room or a house; rather, it is a concept which results from experimentation. It is not surprising, therefore, that Bachelard begins his book by rejecting the preconceived notion of a space within which substances are located.

This traditional emphasis on localization in a fixed space leads to a view of matter as essentially stable. Thus, even though quantum theory implies motion at the heart of matter, the realist continues to insist on the precise location of particles without reference to their momentum. His point of reference is the familiar object in a familiar space, rather than the systematic construction of second approximation. His views apply to large-scale, common reality but they cannot be the basis for the precise knowledge of microphysics. A fundamental lesson of microphysics with respect to space is that nothing valid on localization can be affirmed outside the experimental circumstances of localization. It is precisely this primacy of the means of knowing which requires that the *experiment* of space precede the *experience* of space. Here, Heisenberg's principle has put into mathematical form the basic variables of the experiment of localization and these contradict the Cartesian intuition of space as the dominant characteristic of an immutable substance. For the microphysicist, "touching a body is as metaphorical as touching a heart."[10]

What is stable, what can be "touched" or manipulated, is not space and the objects within it but the mathematical organization of the experiment itself. It is the organization of objectivity by means of mathematical operators "which has stability, permanence, determination, coherence, in short, all the characteristics that are ordinarily attributed to reality" *(EEPC,* 86). Yet Bach-

elard, in an apparent effort to avoid slipping from philosophical
realism to philosophical idealism, is careful to point out that
mathematical symbols are not merely abstract constructions; they
have as their ultimate function a program of experimentation.
Their success "makes them turn from the past to the future of
thought, from the summary to the program" (*EEPC,* 95). Thus
a mathematical operator "is a plan for the actualization of mathematical laws" (*EEPC,* 98–99). Its origin and its activity are
rational; its application serves to "order a more or less amorphous
reality" (*EEPC,* 98).

It does so not through description but through the organized
convergence of probabilities, for "the microphysical experiment
does not translate a reality; it actualizes a chance" (*EEPC,* 102).
In doing so, of course, it transcends the naive spatial experience
of philosophical realism and creates, through the experiment, a
new, informed experience of space. Yet, even here, one cannot
speak of a permanently fixed experience of space. For the origins
of this informed experience are theoretical, and with each change
in theory there is likely to be a change in the experience of space.
"One could almost say; to each new theory, a new space" (*EEPC,*
123).

In fact, the experience of space in microphysics reveals the close
interplay of the rational and the concrete in contemporary science
that Bachelard underscores from the beginning of his epistemological work. Previously, this interaction led him to argue for
a flexible, open rationalism. Such a consequence is as justified
here as it was when he had considered relativity for, as he points
out, "a new discovery made on the structure of space or time
always brings about a reaction in the structure of our mind"
(*EEPC,* 138). The new scientific discoveries on space are of such
fundamental consequence that they indeed bring about a new
scientific mind. Stressing the changes in the reasoning process
that they require, Bachelard urges a " 'Copernican revolution' of
abstraction" (*EEPC,* 139). Such a revolution would complement
the "Copernican revolution of empiricism" (*NES,* 157) which he
had previously attributed to the central role of second approxi-

mation in contemporary science. Together they would reflect both the interaction of the rational and the real as well as the radical, projective nature of the new scientific mind.

The Psychoanalysis of Objective Knowledge

Scattered throughout Bachelard's books on the new scientific mind are occasional reminders of the pedagogical value of particular approaches to knowledge. This concern with developing young minds is stepped up in *La Formation de l'esprit scientifique* (1938), where his intention is not only to draw philosophical conclusions from the activities of contemporary science but actually to promote scientific thinking. Thus we are reminded that the French noun *formation* is related to the English adjective "formative." What is at stake here is nothing less than the proper development of the scientific mind. Yet this should not be taken in the excessively literal sense of "training." Rather, Bachelard is intent upon tracing this development historically and pointing out pitfalls to be avoided in attempting to exercise these new powers of thought. In this respect, his subtitle, indicating a *Contribution to a Psychoanalysis of Objective Knowledge,* is very suggestive. Borrowing only the broadest outlines of Freudian psychoanalysis, Bachelard attempts to eradicate elements from a common intellectual past which may block objective knowledge. There is no abandonment of epistemological concerns here, only a shift to their practical consequences—an attempt both to elucidate and to improve the process of scientific thought.

The point of departure, once again, is the necessary correlation of abstraction and physical reality in scientific thought. Having apparently been achieved in earlier science (Descartes, Newton, Fresnel), this correlation is eventually found wanting because it is based on a naive spatial realism and fails to account for deeper relationships than those of the familiar geometry of everyday space and phenomena. But in moving from the primacy of description to the primacy of construction, the science of second approximation gradually discards a relatively visual geometric thought in favor of complete abstraction. The historian of science may study this evolution neutrally, treating all ideas as "facts" in the historical development of science. But, Bachelard points out,

the epistemologist—different in this respect from the historian—must underscore fertile ideas from among all the attainments of a period. For him, the idea must have more than a proof of existence, it must have a destiny in thought. We will not hesitate, therefore, to consider as an error—or as a useless thought, which is not far from being the same thing—any truth that is not part of a general system, any experiment, even an accurate one, whose affirmation remains unrelated to a method of general experimentation, any observation, no matter how real and positive, which is announced within a false perspective of verification.[11]

Because Bachelard concludes that science has a destiny of abstraction, he must consider that, epistemologically, any impediment to the process of abstraction is an error. He had signaled the dangers of such obstructions as early as *La Connaissance approchée,* but they now move to center stage as he examines the development of the scientific mind by focusing systematically on what he calls the "epistemological obstacle."

The Epistemological Obstacle

"For a scientific mind," Bachelard insists, "all knowledge is an answer to a question. If there has been no question, there cannot be any scientific knowledge" (*FES,* 14). Accumulated learning and breadth of culture have no function here, for it is the sense of problem that allows the scientist to increase his knowledge, which in turn permits him to ask new questions. Any knowledge that is not questioned or that does not lead to further questions, any notion that blocks the fundamental questioning activity of science, is an epistemological obstacle. To analyze such obstacles historically, to ferret them out of the practice of contemporary education, is both to recognize and to promote the openness and dynamism necessary to the practice of science. "More precisely, to reveal epistemological obstacles is to help establish the rudiments of a psychoanalysis of reason" (*FES,* 19). Just as conventional psychoanalysis attempts to free the suppressed personality by releasing it from the shackles of the subconscious, so too does the "psychoanalysis of reason" attempt to free the scientific mind from the various irrationalisms that obstruct it. The "subconscious" in the case of science is buried not only in the past of the individual scientist, but in the collective past of science itself, in its history.

Bachelard identifies three specific ages of scientific thought: (1) *the prescientific period,* including classical antiquity and the sixteenth through much of the eighteenth century, (2) *the scientific period,* ranging from the late eighteenth to the beginning of the twentieth century, and (3) *the era of the new scientific mind,* beginning precisely in 1905 with Einstein's relativity. [12] While these divisions may have historical validity, they do not fully reflect the psychology of the researcher who may still be harboring unwittingly attitudes that belong to an earlier period of science. "Even in the new man, there remain vestiges of the old man" (*FES,* 7), warns Bachelard. It is precisely in such traces of former outlooks that all epistemological obstacles are to be found. Indeed, one reason they can so effectively impede knowledge is that at one time, in an earlier state of the development of science, they may have been quite effective in advancing knowledge, but when methods, or even attitudes that once worked, not only are no longer effective but actually block the further advancement of scientific knowledge, they must be identified as epistemological obstacles and eradicated from the scientific process.

Since the Renaissance, for example, great strides were made in science when the researcher learned to depend on empirical observation and to respond to his curiosity about the natural world around him. In the eighteenth century such immediate curiosity became more widespread as cultured amateur scientists tried their hand at solving some of the mysteries of nature, at asking *why* things were so. Yet many serious scientists had already discarded such broad questions in order to concentrate on *how* phenomena occurred, to reduce experiments to their simplest elements. Where the response to an immediately accessible nature had once been quite useful, it now prevented the sense of problem necessary for reduction to take place. Too often, many amateurs of the eighteenth century were more interested in the picturesque aspects of a phenomenon than in attempting to understand its laws.

This imagistic aspect of the prescientific era occasionally continues to interfere with the proper development of the scientific mind when, for example, a teacher unduly emphasizes the startling visual effects of an experiment, or when "explanations" rely on imagery rather than on conceptual abstraction. "A teacher cannot be urged too much to go constantly from the laboratory table to the blackboard in order to extract as quickly as possible the abstract from the concrete" (*FES*, 40), Bachelard advises. First experience is an epistemological obstacle because it substitutes subjective imagery for a rational experiment that relates one phenomenon to another; "what is most immediate in first experience is still ourselves" (*FES*, 46).

But just as a once useful immediate empiricism can become an impediment to further knowledge, so too can the reductive process which supplants it. Where the former can err by giving undue emphasis to what is singular in a phenomenon, the latter can prevent scientific progress by locking thought into certain general laws. For instance, laws indicating that all bodies fall or that all rays of light travel in a straight line were once useful by comparison to previous faulty knowledge, but, in the context of Einstein's theories, they no longer lead to new discoveries and may even prevent those theories and their later confirmation from being adequately understood. In a science of successive approximations, it is no longer possible to separate knowledge of the general from the circumstances in which that knowledge is made possible. As Bachelard emphasizes repeatedly, a close interaction of theory and application is basic to contemporary science. Generalization can prevent the development of science by emphasizing theory without regard to the conditions of its application. A counterpart to the obstacle of immediacy which sins in the other direction, it is an epistemological obstacle because it imposes a priori categories on scientific thought. Its manifestations include not only unwarranted generalization and mere classification but the presumption of universal unity and the reduction of rational knowledge to what is useful.

Like the first two, the remaining obstacles analyzed by Bachelard err by being either excessively concrete or unjustifiably
abstract. Still at work is his underlying definition of knowledge,
which is much less influenced by past scientific practice than by
the activity of the new scientific mind. Any practice or attitude
that prevents the necessary dialectic of abstract reason and physical
reality is seen as an epistemological obstacle. Yet, considering
Bachelard's emphasis on the rational activity of science, it should
not be surprising that most obstacles are impediments to the
reasoning process rather than to its application.

The scientist, Bachelard admonishes, must be wary of the
seduction of words and the images they evoke. Recalling that in
the eighteenth century the image of a sponge or "sponginess" was
thought to offer an adequate explanation of the properties of air
or of some characteristics of electricity, he points out that, in
fact, the expression merely substituted for an explanation. Bachelard maintains that this substitution of expression for explanation, of images for concepts, is a threat to science: "The danger
of immediate metaphors for the development of the scientific
mind is that they are not always images that disappear; they
stimulate autonomous thought; they tend to be completed, to
be fulfilled in the realm of the image" (*FES,* 81). Yet, since all
his examples are drawn from the eighteenth century, Bachelard
is unable to demonstrate any interference with the activity of
contemporary science. One may easily grant that such a danger
exists for the developing mind of a child first exposed to science,
but the interest of the "verbal obstacle" remains largely historical.
Today, as Bachelard indicates, the image is used *after* the concept,
as an illustration, not as an explanation.

Related to the verbal obstacle, which "explains" by expressing,
is the more pervasive prescientific practice of "explaining" a phenomenon by reference to a supposed underlying substance. "One
of the clearest symptoms of the substantialist seduction is the
accumulation of adjectives on the same noun" (*FES,* 111). The
adjectives attempt to offer an explanation of the object by pointing
to a deeper, hidden substance behind the appearance. In an early
suggestion that imagination and dreaming are closely related,

Bachelard stresses that the *"myth of the interior* is one of the most difficult of the fundamental processes of unconscious thought to exorcise. In our opinion interiorization belongs to the realm of dreams" *(FES,* 101). By juxtaposing adjectives in no particular rational order, prescientific references to hidden substance encourage the view that reality is ultimately unknowable through rational processes. Moreover, such adjectives assign a subjective value to substance which, in Bachelard's view, explains the realist's attachment to substance as something fundamental and irreducible.

In the first of a long list of loose adaptations from psychoanalysis, Bachelard invents the term "Harpagon complex" *(FES,* 132) to describe this attitude. Like the gold of Molière's famous miser, substance for the realist is wealth to be cherished and preserved at all costs. As Bachelard sees it, such a complex must be "psychoanalyzed" in order to free the mind from the irrationalism of the substantialist obstacle. Yet the task is far from easy since the prescientific realist has learned partially to rectify superstition through reason in order to maintain a cultural heritage that gives continuity to acquired learning at the expense of experimental knowledge. "The mixture of learned and experimental thought is, in fact, one of the greatest obstacles to the scientific mind" *(FES,* 133).

To the epistemological obstacles that stem from an insufficiently rational approach to *physical* reality must be added those obstacles whose source of irrationalism is to be found in an unwarranted prejudice for life. Not unlike the substantialist obstacle's undue emphasis on depth, the animist obstacle reflects the disposition of the prescientific mind to explain physical reality by reference to the hidden and often mysterious processes of the body, including particularly digestion and the sexual urge. The prescientific mind does not seek abstraction but concrete, individualized experience, so that the source of animism continues to be naive realism. In its early, prescientific stages, for example, "chemistry claims to learn by scrutinizing the phenomena of digestion" *(FES,* 173) while "electricity . . . is sexualized all the more for being mysterious" *(FES,* 201). Like substantialism, animism gives value to what is hidden. Because it, too, reacts to the subjective qualities of phenomena, it must be viewed as an obstacle to knowledge.

Yet objectivity is not necessarily guaranteed by relying on quantitative thought. Just as generalization can become an impediment to knowledge when it is insufficiently tested by reference to physical reality, rigorous measurement can become an epistemological obstacle when it is unjustifiably precise. "In the eighteenth century," Bachelard points out, "a wholly gratuitous excess of precision is the rule" (*FES,* 214). The true scientist, on the other hand, learns to differentiate between what is negligible and what is not. He learns that when precision goes beyond experimental data it is a "determination of nothingness" (*FES,* 214). Unwarranted precision impedes knowledge by losing sight of what, for Bachelard, is an essential aspect of contemporary science, namely that any phenomenon is the result of the degree of approximation. It is meaningless to attempt to measure precisely traits that go beyond the scientist's means of detection. Where the realist measures because he has the object at hand, the scientist is careful to describe the method of measurement. Thus Bachelard claims that "the scientist believes in the *realism* of measurement more than in the *reality* of the object" (*FES,* 213). Objectivity, for Bachelard, is the affirmation of a method that is mindful of the limits imposed on measurement by the order of magnitude.

Pedagogical Consequences

Bachelard's historical overview of the obstacles to knowledge allows him to identify essential characteristics of objectivity and to draw conclusions for modern pedagogical practice. A methodological self-consciousness is at the heart of scientific objectivity because, historically, as Bachelard has shown, science has progressed by going beyond the all-too-obvious lessons of immediate physical reality and by learning to adjust its methods to the reality being studied. Objectivity does not depend on direct access to the object but on a careful construction of the experiment, subject to the *"social control"* (*FES,* 241) of other informed observers. The researcher must therefore account to other scientists who may detect what, in terms of existing knowledge, appears to be an error in his conclusions. In Bachelard's view, it is precisely when such "errors" are then proven to be correct that existing knowledge is challenged and science progresses. When they occur in the context of an active science, errors can be positive—a notion Bachelard will explore more fully in *La Philosophie du non* [The Philosophy of No].

As Bachelard sees it, the history and current practice of science is not without its consequences, both educational and more broadly cultural, for contemporary France. It is clear, for instance, that young scientific minds must learn to understand the key role played by method in science. Teaching experimental *results* is not enough and may all too often lead the student to interpret those results by reference to subjective imagery, to "that supremacy of the resulting image over the calculation that must explain it" (*FES*, 235), so frequent in the history of science. On the other hand, Bachelard is convinced that the communal activity of science makes science easy to teach and ought, therefore, to be emphasized. Students, he proposes, should be prodded "to an awareness of group reason, in other words, to the instinct of social objectivity." He bemoans the fact that, in French schools, "the opposite instinct of *originality*" is encouraged "without noticing the false character of this originality learned in literary disciplines" (*FES*, 244).

The common reasoning process of science relies neither on subjectivity nor on arbitrary authority. Science is, in itself, a continuous learning activity, both for the teacher and the student. Bachelard insists that, "for objective science to be fully educational, its teaching should be socially active. It is a great mistake of general education to establish the inflexible, one-way relationship of teacher to pupil. In our opinion, the fundamental principle of a *pedagogy* of the objective attitude is as follows: *He who is taught must teach.* An education that one receives without transmitting it develops minds without dynamism, without self-criticism" (*FES*, 244). To require such disciplined thinking of students is to make them aware through experience of the necessary interplay between empiricism and rationalism in science. As Bachelard points out, *"a lesson received is psychologically an empiricism; a lesson given is psychologically a rationalism"* (*FES*, 246). He urges teachers to follow the model of an active science and replace lessons with discoveries.

More broadly, Bachelard maintains that scientific thought, when it becomes a way of life, is "psychologically formative" (*FES*, 250). With this nuance he shifts from his primary concern with the development of the scientific mind to a consideration of its benefits. The practice of scientific thinking, Bachelard suggests, can teach us to think objectively "against the object" (*FES*, 250), to "resist first reflexion" (*FES*, 250–251), and to adopt the dynamism required by the pursuit of objective truth. He is persuaded that a fuller integration of science and society would be beneficial to both—to society because it would reduce irrationalism and arbitrariness, to science because it would encourage attitudes of dynamic objectivity so necessary to the further advancement of knowledge. The scientific mind at work makes it clear that "School goes on for a lifetime" and requires an inversion of social interests so that "Society will be made for School and not School for Society" (*FES*, 252).

The Epistemological Profile

By the time he published *The Philosophy of No: A Philosophy of the New Scientific Mind* in 1940, Bachelard had already begun his work on the literary imagination. Yet, as the subtitle indicates, the *Philosophy of No* is closely related to the three works just examined, for it also considers the implications of contemporary science for reason and philosophy. It is an attempt to correct what Bachelard views as the shortcomings of traditional philosophy which judges science from the perspective of fixed, absolute a priori categories.

Faithful to his belief that philosophy must learn from science, Bachelard begins with a consideration of the epistemological problems raised by the concept of mass. As in *La Formation de l'esprit scientifique,* his approach is initially historical. He briefly traces the development of the concept from early animist notions, where the idea of mass is "understood" subjectively, through stages of realism and positivism, where instrumental measurements are first attempted, to various degrees of rationalism. Here mathematical laws initially relate the idea of mass to other concepts (force and acceleration), but ultimately such laws disclose the internal rationality of the concept of mass as well as the interaction of various rational constructs. In short, Bachelard's historical overview of the concept of mass reveals its increasingly rational character.

To one already familiar with Bachelard's earlier works, this increasing rationality of a concept over time is not particularly surprising. What is new in *The Philosophy of No* is the clarification Bachelard brings to the question of how the history of a concept can interfere with objective knowledge in the mind of a particular thinker. For Bachelard insists that an individual philosopher or scientist incorporates into his own notion of mass, or any other similar concept, something of its historical stages. In other words, various philosophies, ranging from realism to rationalism, not only make up the history of a concept but are an active part of its psychology at any given time. It is possible, Bachelard maintains, to outline a spectrum of philosophical attitudes at work when an individual thinker formulates a concept, but this spectrum, or "epistemological profile," must meet two tests: (1) it "must always be relative to a designated concept" and (2) it can be valid "only for one specific mind which undertakes to examine itself at a particular stage of its culture."[13] By limiting the epistemological profile both synchronically and diachronically in this way, Bachelard hopes to avoid slipping into vague generalizations that would make the notion useless for philosophy.

Yet, while he characteristically shuns the arrogance of general philosophical pronouncements, Bachelard is not able to elude vagueness altogether. Despite attempts to limit the profile to time, person, and circumstance, the degree of influence of any particular philosophy in the spectrum must ultimately be determined subjectively. This is quite evident when Bachelard gives as examples of the epistemological profile his own concepts of mass and energy. Both concepts are plotted on a chart showing the influence of five philosophical stages in the rationalization of each notion: (1) naive realism, (2) clear positivist empiricism, (3) classical rationalism of rational mechanics, (4) complete rationalism (relativity), and (5) discursive rationalism. The utility of such a graph is not in its precision but in the *relative* importance it gives to each stage. Thus, for Bachelard, naive realism plays a much more important role in his personal notion of energy than it does in his concept of mass, while the influence of classical rationalism continues to be great in both concepts.

When charted in this way, the epistemological profile includes epistemological obstacles that had to be overcome on the way to increased rationalism but which nevertheless continue to influence thought in certain circumstances. It illustrates graphically Bachelard's view that earlier attitudes are transcended and not abandoned altogether when a concept is further rationalized. Rather than an achieved result, rationalism is shown to be a process which gives cohesion to scientific thought through "philosophical pluralism" (*PN*, 41).

Non-Aristotelian Logic

Epistemological profiles, for all their particular differences, consistently demonstrate that, if contemporary scientific concepts are to be taken into account, a "dialectical" process—in which juxtaposed rational systems are transcended by a new rationality—is necessarily at the heart of modern scientific thought. The traditional Aristotelian logic of everyday experience, where objects appear stable, cannot apply to the realm of "intellectualized representation" of contemporary science, for, as Bachelard reminds us: "The world in which we think is not the world in which we live" (*PN*, 95). The second-approximation world of scientific thought inaugurates a non-Aristotelian logic which transcends the established Aristotelian logic of immediate reality without denying that logic's applicability to the realm of first approximation.

Non-Aristotelian logic is the philosophical counterpart to non-Newtonian physics and non-Euclidian geometry. Like contemporary physical science and mathematics, it does not negate former logic absolutely; rather, it reorganizes knowledge on a broader base. This broader logic makes possible the pluralistic philosophy revealed by an epistemological profile. Such a philosophy is a dialectical one, a "philosophy of no" in which, as with contemporary science and mathematics, thesis and antithesis are not contradictory but complementary. The philosophy of no, instructed by the epistemological profile, recognizes that a fruitful negation maintains contact with the first formation of a concept. "Generalization by negation must include what it denies" (*PN*, 117).

According to this philosophy, an adequate understanding of a contemporary scientific concept, such as the atom of modern physics, requires that its epistemological profile be made explicit. Otherwise, naive images or other epistemological obstacles which have not been subjected to the criticism of "polemical reasoning" (*PN*, 119) may inadvertently continue to hold sway and reduce the objectivity of the concept. As always, objectivity for Bachelard results from increasing rationalism, from what he now calls "surrationalism":

By means of dialectics and criticisms, surrationalism somehow determines a *super-object*. The super-object is the result of a critical objectification, of an objectivity which only retains that part of the object which it has criticized. As it appears in contemporary microphysics, the atom is the very type of the super-object. In its relationships with images, the super-object is essentially the non-image. Intuitions are very useful: they serve to be destroyed. By destroying its original images, scientific thought discovers its original laws. (*PN*, 119)

The philosophy of no, therefore, is the philosophy of a non-Aristotelian surrationalism which, despite its name, assumes a more limited role than traditional, immediate, a priori reasoning. This new rationalism recognizes that "the variations of reasoning are numerous now in the geometric and physical sciences" and that "reason . . . must obey science" (*PN*, 123). Unlike the absolute reason of the past, the philosophy of no is not merely a philosophy. When required to do so by the rational constructs of objective science, it is prepared dialectically to transcend former notions. It is prepared to say no and be right, rather than to stand fast and risk becoming irrelevant.

The Dialectic of Reason and Matter

The Philosophy of No was published only a few months before Bachelard went to the Sorbonne in the fall of 1940 to assume his post as professor of the history and philosophy of science. For the next eight years he was to busy himself with his work on the imagination of water, air, and earth. While he wrote a few articles and reviews relating to the philosophy of science during this period, it was not until 1949, with *Le Rationalisme appliqué,* that Bachelard focused once again on epistemological issues. From then until the eve of his retirement from the Sorbonne, he published what can best be described as an epistemological trilogy which, in addition to *Le Rationalisme appliqué,* includes *L'Activité rationaliste de la physique contemporaine* (1951) and *Le Matérialisme rationnel* (1953).

As the titles indicate, these three books examine the fundamental relationship of rationalism and empiricism in contemporary science. In addition, all three explore pedagogical issues which had been raised in *La Formation de l'esprit scientifique.* They are, in short, a continuation of Bachelard's analysis of the new scientific mind. As he points out in *L'Activité rationaliste de la physique contemporaine,* his role "is not to instruct [the] reader scientifically, but rather to make evident the philosophical values of science" (*ARPC,* 267–68). But the trilogy expands the scope of earlier epistemological works in one important respect: it examines *in detail* the ontological questions raised by science to which Bachelard had given only passing attention until now. That one of the principal "philosophical values" should now include the *ontological* value of contemporary science, suggests that Bachelard's increasingly metaphysical exploration of the imagination of elements during the intervening years has had an effect, not on the conclusions he draws (Bachelard consistently recognizes the particularities of science), but on the questions he asks.

In *Le Rationalisme appliqué* Bachelard recalls that contemporary physics dialectically joins abstract mathematics and concrete experiment in an applied rationalism which, philosophically, represents a mid-point between idealism and realism. This "technical materialism," an expression Bachelard sometimes substitutes for "applied rationalism," corresponds to a reality rectified and reconstructed by algebraic abstraction. Its ontology is discursive rather than immediate because being is *confirmed* in the context of a rational community rather than *affirmed* individually. Such a communal confirmation gives rise to well-defined areas within which certain ideas prevail by making possible additional discoveries. Bachelard finds it more accurate to speak of "regional rationalisms"[14] rather than of the unified rationalism of traditional philosophy when the applied rationalism of science is taken into account. This applied rationalism is generalized not by summarizing common elements in the regional rationalisms of various theories but by integrating and organizing them for instruction as well as by recognizing the multiple, axiomatic structures within which contemporary scientific knowledge progresses.

Insisting on the combined rational and technical nature of scientific activity in *L'Activité rationaliste de la physique contemporaine,* Bachelard examines the regional rationalism of modern theories of light. Recalling that wave mechanics lead to simultaneous intuitions of particles and waves, he points out that this does not justify attributing absolute ontological value either to particles or to waves. Rather, their provisional ontological status is conditioned by technical experiment and is a statement of probability about a plurality of events including both waves and particles. In contemporary physics the real is essentially dynamic, Bachelard reminds us, so that particles should not be viewed as objects at rest but as states in a dynamic transformation. It becomes more appropriate, therefore, to speak of "dynamology" (*ARPC,* 206) rather than ontology when drawing philosophical conclusions from contemporary physics. "It is energy that becomes the fundamental ontological notion of any modern doctrine of matter" (*ARPC,* 188).

The notion of an applied rationalism reflecting the abstract-concrete dialectic of contemporary physics is complemented in *Le Matérialisme rationnel,* by the increasing rationalization of matter in modern chemistry. Unlike the "natural" materialism attacked by idealist philosophy, the rational materialism of chemistry shares with physics a position midway between the idealist and realist extremes. Bachelard recalls that each extreme has led to erroneous views of reality as either substance or form. The applied rationalism of chemistry, on the other hand, can be described as a long and arduous task of "restrictive ontology"[15] which avoids both the temptation of cosmic idealism and of naive realism. Less encompassing than the ontology of traditional metaphysics, it has the virtue, in Bachelard's eyes, of recognizing that the reality of contemporary chemistry incorporates a method.

Thus, despite a greater attention to ontological questions in the trilogy, Bachelard maintains his basic position that philosophy must avoid imposing a priori categories upon science, that it must learn from science. He does not proceed from the premise that science will necessarily lead to ontology. But he also avoids the opposite, equally dogmatic presupposition that science can have no metaphysical relevance. The ontological questions may be asked, but only if they respect the primacy of epistemology inherent in the practice of science. As Bachelard sees it, and on this point he is consistent, whatever can be affirmed about reality in science depends upon how that reality is known. In science there can be no ontological finality.

Chapter Four

Fragmentation and the Temptation of Ontology

As Bachelard explores the revolutionary character of the new scientific mind throughout the 1930s, he is compelled to emphasize the increasing rationalism of contemporary science and the corresponding reduction of philosophical realism—of notions such as substance, essential quality, and fixity. Yet, in contrast to the fragmentation of space and matter represented by theories of the atom as well as to a corresponding fractioning of time, Bachelard is drawn, imperceptibly at first, to the integrative nature of aesthetic activity. While it is often assumed that this transformation takes place in the late 1930s with the publication of *The Psychoanalysis of Fire,* there are strong indications that this "conversion to the imaginary"[1] begins early in the decade when Bachelard, influenced by his friend and colleague, Gaston Roupnel, with whom he shared an appreciation of the materiality of country life, published *L'Intuition de l'instant* (1932), a sympathetic philosophical assessment of Roupnel's temporal theories.

The modulation in Bachelard's outlook is so gradual and discontinuous that most works of the 1930s are still overwhelmingly epistemological. Yet Bachelard makes several attempts during this period to deal with space, time, and matter as they are experienced, rather than as they are experimentally known. Thus, in *Les Intuitions atomistiques* (1933), he explores at length earlier notions of the localization of matter, although these will be quickly dismissed four years later in the first chapter of *L'Expérience de l'espace dans la physique contemporaine.* But, in his intermittent transition from the philosophy of science to a concern with aesthetic creation, it is the fragmentation of time which most suggests ontological values, and it is especially in dealing with the question of time, both in *L'Intuition de l'instant* and in the later *Dialectique de la durée,* that Bachelard allows himself the greatest freedom from epistemological concerns. In order adequately to understand Bachelard's transformation, therefore, it is best to avoid strict chronology and begin with *Les Intuitions atomistiques* before considering the more evident temptations of ontology in the two essays on time. In *Les Intuitions atomistiques* the epistemological outlook characteristic of his early work is still quite strong.

The Atom and the Seduction of Realism

Les Intuitions atomistiques: Essai de classification outlines various intuitions of the atom, first in antiquity and then from the seventeenth century to the present. Because these notions are so different over time, Bachelard must distinguish between two broad categories of intuitions: those grounded in realism and those based on the rational organization of knowledge. Within these two divisions, especially within the second, intuitions are differentiated further as Bachelard traces the evolution of the idea of the atom toward contemporary objectivity. But, while much of his examination is chronological, he is less intent upon writing a history of atomism than in revealing how synthetic and analytic intuitions of the atom must eventually complement each other if they are to lead to a dialectic of reason and observation necessary to an objective understanding of the atom.

Roughly foreshadowing what was to become, some seven years later, the "epistemological profile," Bachelard's scheme proposes to gain an appreciation of the philosophical dimensions of contemporary atomic theory by classifying atomic intuitions whenever they occur: "our goal is to underline the intuitive traits of atomistic doctrines, to show also how an intuition becomes an argument, how finally an argument seeks an intuition to clarify itself. . . . Under these conditions, we will therefore assume the right to borrow examples from very different moments of philosophical evolution."[2] Such license allows Bachelard to classify the complex of intuitions regarding the atom in light of

modern science where, as is consistently the case in his epistemology, "we will see the efforts of reason and experiment converge" (*IA,* 14). Yet fully the first half of his monograph is
devoted to the metaphysical characteristics of naive atomistic
realism and its "occasions for imagining" (*IA,* 13), even though
his purpose is not to explore the imagination but to argue against
its dark enchantments.

In "The Metaphysics of Dust," a chapter title curiously more
befitting the phenomenology of his later books on the imagination
than an epistemological essay, Bachelard indicates that initial
intuitions of the atom were inspired by the sight of dust particles
suspended in midair. Early atomistic intuitions were visual; they
represented minuscule particles of matter and emptiness in the
same gaze. While Bachelard is careful to point out that classical
philosophy was initially less impressed by such sensual experiences, he does relate this notion of the "atom" isolated in the
void to the idea that the atom "is easily taken as the archetype
of the independent and immutable object" (*IA,* 41). Because it
is thought of as irreducible, it is also viewed as the precise cause
of that quality associated with a specific substance. For, as he
recalls, naive realism explains everything by means of a single
"epistemological function" (*IA,* 46), which he labels the *"realistic
function"* (*IA,* 47). Such a function refers an observable quality
to a substance, so that the object is considered to *possess* a particular
property. The atom, therefore, becomes the irreducible kernel
of that quality.

Thus, realistic atomism, "contrary to the ideal of modern scientific thought, . . . tends to reduce the *laws* of the phenomenon
to the *properties* of substances . . . [so that] explanation consists
of establishing a tautology which goes from substance to the
qualities that characterize it" (*IA,* 59). The composed or struc-
tured reality of modern science would be incomprehensible to a
realist for whom all diversity stems from the essence of things
rather than from their combinations. Yet this resistance of realistic
atomism to any form of exterior, rational construct, this explanation of properties by reference to the center, as it becomes more
sophisticated, eventually replaces the intuition of the atom as a

substantial phenomenon with a *new* intuition of atomic dyna-mism. This is particularly so for Newton himself, who, "protected by mathematical precautions, has personally escaped this realistic seduction" (*IA,* 63). Because the atom's cohesion is now explained by dynamic internal forces of attraction, it can no longer be seen as the smallest particle, as an essential cause. "The method of explanation thus automatically ruins the atom as a means of explanation" (*IA,* 65–66).

As the atom loses its inherent spatial dimension, Bachelard insists, it is conceived as a mathematical point. "Thus we end up with an atomism where the internal and the external touch so to speak" (*IA,* 66). The result is a schematic, mathematical explanation from the outside that had been rejected in earlier realistic intuitions. "It is from the relative position of atoms in space that all actions, and, consequently, all properties of atoms derive. We thus come to a mathematical physics that gets away from the traditional principles of atomism" (*IA,* 66). In short, the explanation from within, in which properties are assigned to the atom, initially favored by traditional realism, becomes math-ematical and leads from an early visual intuition of the atom to a geometric intuition in which the atom derives its dynamic properties from its position in relation to other atoms.

Such an outcome may easily overlook the "very great variety" (*IA,* 68) of realistic atomism, all of which falls between two extremes: "truly prodigal realistic atomism which assigns all the properties of the phenomenon to the atom itself and the most restrained realistic atomism possible which fixes a single property as essential to the atom" (*IA,* 68). Bachelard maintains that realistic atomism can be positioned on a spectrum by reference to the question of the composition of phenomena: "Between these extreme positions, one could easily classify the solutions to the problem of phenomenal composition in order of increasing com-plexity" (*IA,* 69). Simply put, this is possible because, for prod-igal atomism, all attributes are at the level of the atom so that the question of a phenomenon's composition is meaningless, while it is fundamental for restrained atomism where properties are the result of combinations of atoms. As we move along the spectrum, therefore, we encounter an increasingly synthetic basis of reality, one which approaches the constructive reality of contemporary science. But, Bachelard insists, it is not easy for the prescientific mind to discard its illusions and to accept the possibility that a composed phenomenon can generate a reality different from its component parts. "It is therefore difficult to dismiss the seduction of an immediate ontology" (*IA*, 71), although it is necessary if the problems of atomism are to be elucidated by modern science and if we are to move from realistic to rationalistic intuitions.

Toward an Axiomatic Atomism

The transformation from atomistic realism to atomistic rationalism is a gradual one. For, even when atomistic intuitions are grounded in reason and related to philosophical idealism, the temptations of realism remain. It may well be that for positivism all "philosophical intuitions are relegated to the rank of subordinate images" (*IA*, 90), but, as Bachelard shows, the hypotheses of several nineteenth-century scientists gradually come to be taken as empirical observation when their verifications converge. Historically, Bachelard concludes, positivism is an intermediate step between realism and rationalism.

In the work of the late-nineteenth-century philosopher of science Arthur Hannequin, Bachelard perceives a Kantian idealism which leads to the intuition that "atomism does not reside in the examined object, that, consequently, it is in no way realistic, but that, on the contrary, this atomism is dependent upon the method of examination" (*IA*, 108). Such a mathematically inspired atomism seems "far from any ontological characteristic" (*IA*, 111). Yet, in the final analysis, this idealism gives way to a continuing, though subtle temptation of realism. As Bachelard indicates, Hannequin encounters the "temptation to posit the real beneath the convergence of relations" (*IA*, 117) when the atom is taken as a *cause* of motion. Just as realism emerges from the convergence of positivistic hypotheses, so too does the equation of geometric and mechanical atomism in Hannequin lead to "an underlying individuality" where appears "the profound being, trace of a poorly exorcised realism" (*IA*, 121).

For Bachelard, therefore, atomism, even idealist atomism, does not fully escape the temptation of ontology until it becomes axiomatic in the early twentieth century. Recalling that contemporary atomism, unlike traditional science, does not search for general principles on the basis of initial observation but begins with principles and only later seeks confirmation in experimental observation, Bachelard alludes to his original definition of knowledge (to describe in order to retrieve) when he points out that in contemporary atomism "we can no longer give a *definition that describes;* at most we can only give a *definition in order to describe"* (*IA,* 133). Unlike the axioms of positivism, which may summarize concepts, the axioms of contemporary atomism, Bachelard asserts, are principles that lead to discoveries. They are not merely descriptive; they are also projective. They need not be seen as real as long as they successfully establish the basis of a construction. Axiomatic atomism avoids the ontological temptation because it "is simply the basis of a construction that alone can claim to attain a reality or a truth" (*IA,* 147).

The atom no longer represents the limits of analysis but rather the most productive source of synthesis. It leads away from everyday reality, from the "illusory character of our first intuitions" (*IA,* 153), toward the rational constructs of contemporary science. Discarding the assumptions of realism, contemporary science, according to Bachelard, views the atom not as an object to be known but as "a center of convergence for technical methods" (*IA,* 154). Its objectivity results from this convergence rather than from direct observation. "Intuitions of the senses must therefore give way to rational intuitions" (*IA,* 160). When this occurs, how we know clearly is more important than what we know; ontology is then rejected in favor of epistemology. But, in the case of the atom at least, this happens only after a very long struggle with the temptations of realism, a struggle which Bachelard allows himself to describe in unusual detail.

The Instant and the Intuition of Time

Published one year before *Les Intuitions atomistiques, L'Intuition de l'instant* (1932) is less an attempt to review intuitions objectively than an essay recounting the subjective experience of certain intuitions of time. The difference is important since it marks Bachelard's first departure from a strictly conceptual method in order to adapt his approach to the subjective experience being examined.[3] Yet the transformation is far from complete: Bachelard's intuition is still very much influenced by scientific knowledge and he continues to be extremely suspicious of philosophical realism. But in attempting "to reconcile the beginning of being and the beginning of thought,"[4] the epistemologist, who that same year also published *Le Pluralisme cohérent de la chimie moderne,* now confronts a decidedly ontological task.

The immediate cause of this shift in emphasis is of course Gaston Roupnel's intuitive study of time and habit entitled *Siloë.*[5] Perhaps it takes the bonds and sympathy of friendship for a philosopher of science like Bachelard to write on a book he himself describes as "the work of a poet" (*II,* 7), but he leaves no doubt that *L'Intuition de l'instant* is meant to "bring to light this new intuition and to show its metaphysical interest" (*II,* 7). Thus, while his approach to the subject is modified, Bachelard's frame of reference remains philosophical.

Significantly, Bachelard treads cautiously in this new terrain. Aware that his usual conceptual approach, if applied strictly, would destroy the very intuition he is trying to examine, Bachelard respects its subjective nature and its lyrical expression by identifying with it in order truly to know it:

We have therefore taken the intuitions of *Siloë* back as close as possible to their source and we have striven to follow in ourself the impetus that these intuitions could give to philosophical thought. For several months they became the setting and the framework of our constructions. After all, an intuition is not proven, it is experienced. And it is experienced by multiplying or even by modifying the conditions of its use. . . . We have thus freely used the intuitions of *Siloë* and finally, more than an objective account, it is our experience of the book that we provide here. (*II,* 8)

In a shift, whose consequence will not be apparent until well after he embarks upon his works on the imagination, Bachelard allows the possibility that knowledge may sometimes be based on experience rather than reason. This is not the only time that he deals with subjective intuitions outside a mathematical framework, but it is the first time he treats such intuitions sympathetically. In his later epistemological works, subjective intuitions, when they do not operate within mathematical constraints, are considered obstacles to knowledge. Here, however, such intuitions are the source of a new kind of experiential knowledge whose validity is tested by adopting the intuitions and extending their application. Bachelard, still very much the epistemologist, does not discard objectivity and reference to science altogether, especially in the early part of his essay. But he does allow himself an unprecedented reliance on subjective experience.

Initially he compares Roupnel's intuitions, in which the fundamental temporal reality is the instant, to the ideas of Henri Bergson, for whom time is ultimately duration.[6] After searching for a compromise between the two positions, Bachelard finally abandons Bergson's point of view when he realizes that it will not withstand the challenge of Einstein's theory. A consequence of that theory is that any length of time is relative to the method of measurement. "For systems in motion, relativity of elapsed time is henceforth a scientific principle" (*II, 30*), so that there is no external, objective support for individual intuitions of duration. On the other hand, Bachelard maintains that *"the well specified instant remains an absolute in Einstein's doctrine. To give it this absolute value, it is enough to consider the instant in its synthetic state, as a point of space-time"* (*II, 30–31*). This interpretation of scientific theory is merely the point of departure, but it is all that is needed for Bachelard confidently to draw certain ontological conclusions. He thus agrees with Roupnel that "time is a reality confined to the instant and suspended between two voids" (*II, 13*). But, influenced by Einstein's theories, Bachelard goes even further in his ontology when he suggests that "we must consider being as a synthesis supported at once by space and time" (*II, 31*).

Moreover, as Bachelard meditates on the operation of will and knowledge, he adds consciousness as a third element of this minimal reality. He is convinced that decision, awareness, and attentiveness all share the intensity of the instant. All are phenomena which affirm a newness in an individual's consciousness at a particular time and place. "Finally, what would best analyze the psychology of will, evidence, and attentiveness, is the point of space-time. . . . It is along this path that we shall be able to effect the fusion of spatial atomism and of temporal atomism. . . . The space-time-consciousness complex is a triple essence atomism" (*II,* 37). But this point of space, time, and consciousness, because it is the atom of our reality, is necessarily isolated. Borrowing from Leibniz, Bachelard describes it as a "monad affirmed in its triple solitude" (*II,* 37), which has no contact with other places, other times, or any other consciousness. Like Roupnel's instant, Bachelard's monad must be utterly isolated in order for it not to be confused with the phenomena of appearance.

Instant, Continuity, and the Aesthetic Solution

Bachelard must therefore relegate the past, the future, and duration in general to a secondary status as a retrospective or prospective, indirect representation of reality and time. Just as in his epistemology Bachelard sees substance as a metaphor of scientific reality rather than as the fundamental physical reality it was once thought to be, he sees duration merely as a representation of time, as an indirect substitute for temporal reality. He associates substance and duration with an assumed preestablished harmony in the world, one which both contemporary science and his own meditation on Roupnel's intuitions have rendered untenable.

Yet, while they may not be the reality of space-time-consciousness, while they may be secondary, the past and the future clearly are part of our experience as our being both continues and evolves over time. Bergson anticipated the problem when he indicated that, if instant follows instant, "there would be nothing but present, no prolongation of the past into the here and now, no evolution, no concrete duration."[7] Having rejected Bergsonian duration and preestablished harmony, Bachelard is nonetheless aware that "it becomes more necessary than ever to show how a non-direct, non-temporal solidarity is manifested in the becoming of being. In short, we must find a principle to replace the hypothesis of preestablished order" (*II*, 60). He finds such a principle in Roupnel's conceptions of habit. The challenge for Bachelard is to demonstrate how habit is possible and how it can explain the continuity of being in the context of intuitions of isolation.

Inspired by Roupnel, Bachelard's solution is to suggest that there is a hierarchy of habits. The primary habit continues former being by renewing it in the instant while "the consequences and the development of this act are committed to subordinate habits" (*II*, 64). Thus habit is synthetic: it combines the innovation of a fresh act, of a beginning, with the permanence of continuity. Bachelard gives the example of the pianist who has acquired many habits of play but who must constantly strive to improve if he does not want to see his acquired technique decline. For the most essential element of habit is inventiveness. It is this innovation, this growth, that gives the full range of possibilities to being while maintaining a continuity.

Thus, the continuity of being, in a kind of coherent pluralism, depends on a sequential rhythm of repeated innovations rather than on passive duration. "A particular habit is a sustained rhythm, where all the acts are repeated while equalizing more or less exactly their value of newness, but without ever losing that dominant characteristic of being a newness" (*II*, 68). Because this dominant habit is fundamentally innovative, it is inconceivable for Bachelard that it would be anything but a conscious process. Instead, an inventive consciousness links discontinuous instants into what Bachelard calls *"chronotropisms"* (*II*, 72), as it tends "toward a more or less rational project" (*II*, 73). The resultant temporal rhythms are both directed and free. They are directed by their tendency toward a project, but they are free by virtue of the conscious innovation of each instant of this temporal rhythm. Thus, Bachelard sees the continuity of being as both rational and aesthetic: "This invitation of habit to pursue the rhythm of well-ordered acts is at bottom an obligation of an almost rational and aesthetic nature. Reasons rather than forces compel us to persevere in being. It is this rational and aesthetic coherence in the superior rhythms of thought that forms the keystone of being" (*II, 74*).

At this point it may appear that Bachelard has shifted ground and has made coherence itself, rather than the isolated instant of space-time-consciousness, the foundation of being. The ambiguity may result in part from the fact that "in *Siloë* time is always taken at once as substance and as attribute" (*II, 89*), so that the rhythmical continuity of habit should actually be seen as an attribute or phenomenon of time rather than as its reality. This is, in fact, exactly what Bachelard argues when he concludes that, "There is only one reality: the instant. Duration, habit, and progress are only groupings of instants, they are the simplest of the phenomena of time. None of these temporal phenomena can have an ontological privilege" (*II, 90*).

Yet the ambiguity remains: either rhythmical habit is merely an attribute, in which case temporal continuity has not been adequately explained, or the sequential rhythms of habit are the "keystone of being," in which case the intuition of being in the instant is invalid. Bachelard offers no logical solution, so that the ambiguity must be seen as a contradiction. As Michel Vadée, referring to the instant, points out, "with this single element that contains all reality, Bachelard must explain the construction of time. Therein resides the metaphysical *contradiction* in which his philosophy is locked."[8] Bachelard's solution, in fact, is not philosophical but aesthetic. As Vadée indicates further, "the idea of rhythm becomes the true content of the idea of time."[9]

Throughout *L'Intuition de l'instant* Bachelard manages to preserve the freedom and newness of the instant on the one hand and rhythmic continuity on the other by comparing being and time to music.[10] Are the notes in an original composition not new and free, yet bound by the structures of the work? As Bachelard puts it in one of his many allusions to music, "the coherence of being . . . is fragile and free like a symphony" (*II, 68*). Music is a particularly appropriate metaphor because its notes are truly instants separated by voids of silence, and it, too, is guided by both aesthetic and rational considerations. Yet it is as difficult to decide if the reality of music is to be found in its notes or in its structures as it is to decide if the reality of time is to be found in the instant or in rhythmic continuity. Because temporal reality is part of an inner experience that is not strictly subject to rational constructs, Bachelard attempts to convey it by reference to an image which is also free from the strictures of logic. In using an image to "explain" in this way, Bachelard may not be faithful to the demands of metaphysics, but he does remain true to Roupnel's intuition. Bachelard's ontology is no more bound by preestablished philosophical categories than his epistemology, when, in his view, the particular circumstances demand flexibility.

Duration and the Temporal Dialectic

Four years after *L'Intuition de l'instant* Bachelard returns to the question of time in *La Dialectique de la durée* (1936). As before, he draws from science, from his own intuitions, and from his reading as he pursues his challenge to Bergson's thesis of duration. In this case, mathematical set theory and quantum mechanics virtually replace relativity as the scientific referents while Roupnel's original influence is now broadened to include other philosophers, particularly a little-known Brazilian philosopher, Lucio Alberto Pinheiro dos Santos, whose ideas correspond remarkably well to Bachelard's evolving preoccupation with the primacy of rhythm.

Bachelard also finds Pinheiro dos Santos's emphasis on individual creation especially congenial. Influenced by the Latin-American "creationist" school,[11] Pinheiro dos Santos holds that individual creative evolution is, in Bachelard's words, "a texture of successes and failures."[12] Because Bachelard regards newness or creation as central to being, in each instant, he concludes that being itself dialectically incorporates an absolute risk of nonbeing which is repeatedly overcome in a rhythmical, temporal duration. This absolute risk and the absolute creation which overcomes it go far beyond Bergson's *élan vital,* where risk is ultimately circumscribed by an underlying and uniformly continuous duration. Bergson's philosophy, according to Bachelard, inappropriately limits the essential, conscious creation of being: "the philosophy of the *élan vital* has not been able to give full significance to what we will call the purely ontological success of being, that is, to the renewed creation of being by itself, in the mental act of consciousness in its entirely gratuitous form, as a resistance to the appeal of suicide, as a triumph over the reduction of nothingness" (*DD,* 6). As Bachelard sees it, the very continuity of being in Bergson, the notion that life's momentum cannot be interrupted except superficially, eliminates the possibility of any consideration of the creativity of being.

For Bachelard, continuity is not an admitted fact, as in Bergson, but a problem. After essentially repudiating Bergson by indicating that "from Bergsonism, we accept almost everything, save continuity" (*DD,* 7), Bachelard sets out to construct continuity, to "develop an essay of discontinuous Bergsonism" (*DD,* 8). His purpose is ontological: to discover the nature of being discursively and with reference to experience. "We demand complete ontological proof, discursive proof of being, detailed ontological experience" (*DD,* 11). Much in the manner of a transcendent science that encompasses and goes beyond earlier errors, Bachelard negates prior positions in order to construct new ones, that is, he dialectically transforms and incorporates former errors into a new thesis. "A clear concept must carry the trace of everything we have refused to include within it" (*DD,* 15), so that, while excluding the imposed continuity of Bergson, Bachelard nevertheless is able to construct continuity through an encompassing set of durations.

Bachelard's initial inspiration is mathematical set theory, which, when loosely applied to the problem of time, can serve as a model of discontinuous reality having a continuous function. "Indeed, we do not recognize the right to impose continuity when we observe discontinuity everywhere . . . especially when we consider that mathematical sets are discontinuous but have the power of continuity" (*DD,* 28). By separating reality and function in this way, Bachelard offers a more philosophically sophisticated solution to the metaphysical contradiction between discontinuity and continuity which had ensnared him in *L'Intuition de l'instant.* Set theory serves him better than relativity in exploring his intuitions of time when he shifts his emphasis from the *reality* of the instant to the *function* of duration.

As a function rather than a reality, duration is, in Bachelard's estimation, the result of separate decisions to act. It is not a passive, underlying continuity, hostile to novelty, but a conduct which is willfully continued:

Thus we are gradually led to separate clearly, from the functional point of view, the will that starts an act from the will that continues it. Before the adjunction of the will to endure, we had only to consider the reflex act, closed-in on the instant, taking its full significance from some spatio-temporal coincidence. On the contrary, thought, reflection, clear will, persistent character give duration to an ephemeral act by teaching how to incorporate appropriate secondary acts. We thus grasp duration in its role as conduct, in its role as action. (*DD,* 40)

The cause of a particular duration may be quite effective, but because it depends on conscious will to continue, it may always be stopped or deviated. A subsequent event is either more or less probable; it is rarely inevitable, so that Bachelard views duration as an "ordinal probability" rather than a necessity. "In other words, we notice that the living being and the thinking being are implicated less in necessities than in probabilities. And this implication reserves some freedoms precisely because it is only a question of ordinal probability . . . [that] inclines without necessitating" (*DD,* 88).

This nondeterministic inclination may remind us of the chronotropism of *L'Intuition de l'instant,* where continuity was attributed to the rhythm of repeated action toward a particular project. But to the model of relativity that inspired such a view has now been added the influence of quantum physics. Relativity had supported Bachelard's phenomenological study of time and had led him to "consider several groupings of instants, several superimposed durations, that maintain various relationships" (*DD,* 90), much in the way a musical composition correlates a variety of rhythmical structures. But, like musical melody, relativity and its "intuitions of motion" (*DD,* 90) had also suggested the possibility of continuity despite multiple durations. In quantum theory, on the other hand, change in quality—that is to say, change in the energy state—rather than motion leads Bachelard to a refinement of his intuition of continuity and duration.

Reinforcing the phenomenological observation that "one never experiences continuous change," Bachelard speculates that "the development of quantum physics will require a conception of discontinuous durations that will not have the linear properties illustrated by our intuitions of continuous trajectories. Qualitative becoming is quite naturally a quantum becoming. It must go through a dialectic, go from the same to the same by going through the other" (DD, 91). Quantum theory takes Bachelard one step further than set theory toward dealing with the metaphysical contradiction between the instant and continuity as he now shifts away from time as a function and returns anew to the question of its ontological status.

Rhythmical Continuity and the Formalizing Consciousness

Quantum theory has introduced discontinuity into the heart of physical reality, so that Bachelard need no longer be hesitant about following his Roupnelian inspired intuition of discontinuous time. Indeed, to do so is quite in keeping with his epistemology, wherein he has maintained all along that philosophy must take its lead from science. If quantum theory, with its discontinuous states of energy, can challenge macrophysical impressions of a continuous flow of energy, is the contradiction between the intuitions of temporal discontinuity and the experience of continuity not of like nature? Just as the increase or decrease in energy appears to be continuous because "quantum leaps" are not detectable at the macrophysical level, so too does time "only appear continuous . . . thanks to the superimposition of several independent times" (DD, 92). Bachelard's interpretation of the temporal consequences of quantum theory thus supports his argument for the discontinuous reality of time while allowing for the *apparent* reality of continuity.

But, if time is discontinuous, it is because human temporal reality perceived phenomenologically necessarily involves consciousness of time. Time, for Bachelard, is neither merely an abstraction nor simply the transformation of space and matter without reference to human experience. It is something that is apprehended mentally in what Alexandre Koyré, referring to Hegel's analysis of time, calls "the spiritual reality of time" (quoted in *DD*, 94). Bachelard maintains that the conscious mental time of human experience and an instinctive, subconscious lived time are superimposed, that mental time can be thought of as perpendicular to the horizontal axis of lived time. "The temporal axis, perpendicular to transitive time, to the time of the world and of matter, is an axis where the self can develop a formal activity" (*DD*, 98).

He characterizes this activity as an effort at "compound idealism" in which the foundation of Cartesian ontology—"*I think therefore I am*"—is subjected to the formalizing power of consciousness. In moving to "*I think that I think, therefore I am*" and, finally, to "*I think that I think that I think,*" we move from "thinking of ourselves as involved in thinking *something* to thinking of ourselves as *someone* who thinks" (*DD*, 99). In other words, these steps, which Bachelard, in good scientific fashion, calls $(cogito)^1$, $(cogito)^2$, and $(cogito)^3$, move a formalizing consciousness along a vertical temporal axis as far away as possible—Bachelard claims he cannot conceive of a $(cogito)^4$!—from the horizontal axis of a material, lived time that has no human significance.[13]

Because the vertical axis of time is increasingly formal, it escapes from the subconscious continuity of lived time; it gives duration through form, it has "*constancies without, however, having a continuity*" (*DD*, 110). The appearance of continuity can only result from a particular, usually distant, perspective; it is never actually experienced. Like durations themselves, it is always metaphorical. Returning to the example of music, Bachelard stresses this metaphorical aspect in what would seem to be the most obvious instance of musical continuity: the melody. "In fact, we must *learn* the continuity of a melody. We do not *hear* it the first time around" (*DD*, 114). Here, too, continuity is metaphorical; it is literally composed of discontinuous elements. In orchestral music we may have an impression of synchronic continuity, yet such an impression does not result from any exact measurement of duration, according to Bachelard, but from the correlation of the various instruments in a *"reciprocal support of rhythms* [where] . . . the conductor's role is to make the players' effort at correlation more conscious" (*DD,* 123). Indeed, "we cannot really separate melody and harmony" (*DD,* 123), for there is a dialectic within the component elements of music. "Musical metaphors would thus be much more appropriate in teaching us temporal dialectics than in giving us images of substantial continuity" (*DD,* 124).

Bachelard's return to music as a model should not blind us to the subtle changes in his intuition of time in *La Dialectique de la durée.* It was, after all, precisely to support the idea of continuity that music had been used in *L'Intuition de l'instant.* But such metaphors are merely illustrations of more fundamental intuitions of time which themselves have evolved. Thus, while preserving the ontological status of the instant in *La Dialectique de la durée,* Bachelard deftly accounts for continuity by underscoring the dialectical nature of temporal rhythms. "A trait is rhythmical if it restores itself " (*DD,* 127), so that both its reality in the instant as well as its continuity through a dialectical process are preserved. By "discovering" the dialectical nature of duration and the corresponding metaphorical aspect of continuity, Bachelard responds phenomenologically to temporal experience without assigning any ontological value to continuity. By being more specific about duration, that is, by pointing out that its rhythm is dialectical rather than merely sequential, he avoids slipping into the metaphysical contradiction of attributing being both to continuity and to the instant. In effect, continuity has been replaced by the multiplicity of duration whose dialectical rhythm supports rather than contradicts the reality of the instant.

Even material time, when analyzed scientifically rather than considered as the unconscious general substructure of life, is only apparently uniform and continuous. Bachelard makes this point particularly forcefully by referring once again to physics which teaches that matter and radiation are transformed one into the other and thus share "undulating rhythmical characteristics"

(*DD*, 130). Matter is not consistent and inert; rather it is based on the rhythmical time of frequencies. As Bachelard dramatically puts it: "Our houses are built with an anarchy of vibrations. We walk on an anarchy of vibrations. We sit on an anarchy of vibrations. The pyramids, whose function is to contemplate the monotonous centuries, are interminable cacophonies" (*DD*, 131). Vibrating frequencies are at the core of existence, so that time in its most fundamental aspect is not uniform continuity but vibration. "Matter exists in a vibrated time and only in a vibrated time" (*DD*, 131). Here, too, continuity is a metaphor.

The universality of temporal vibrations, both in matter and in the nonsequential dialectic of consciousness, prompts Bachelard to examine the precepts of Pinheiro dos Santos's "rhythmanalysis," which seeks to understand and explain both biological and psychological functions on the basis of the fundamentality of rhythms. While Bachelard is fully aware that "the decision of the laboratory" (*DD*, 138) has not been rendered on Pinheiro dos Santos's theories, he nevertheless finds that, "more systematically than psychoanalysis, rhythmanalysis seeks patterns of duality for mental activity. . . . It balances better than psychoanalysis tendencies toward opposite poles" (*DD*, 141). His preferences for Pinheiro dos Santos's speculations may indicate, in part, Bachelard's own unorthodox view of psychoanalysis, but it also certainly reflects his prejudices as a rationalist. Pointing out that "psychoanalysis—as has often been observed—underestimated the conscious and rational life of the mind" (*DD*, 143), he agrees with Pinheiro dos Santos that man has a need to transcend himself. Sublimation should be seen as an upward attraction toward creative activity rather than as a compensation for suppressed impulses. Foreshadowing by two decades a view he will develop in *The Poetics of Space*, Bachelard proclaims that "art is not a last resort for the sexual drive" (*DD*, 141).[14]

Poetry and the Ontological Temptation

Such a conception of creative activity corresponds to the formalizing power of thought along a vertical axis. Not surprisingly,

Bachelard seems to view art primarily in terms of form and thought at this point, and that includes a predilection for the patterned and cerebral poetry of Valéry. In applying temporal dialectics to Valéry's poetry, Bachelard discovers that "it was the ideas that sang" (*DD,* 150). Just a few years after *La Dialectique de la durée,* he is even more specific about the connection among the vertical time of consciousness, the instant, and poetry: "It is in the vertical time of an immobilized moment that poetry finds its specific dynamism."[15]

This view of poetry and time must surely recall Valéry's famous *Graveyard by the Sea,* where the flow of life is suspended in a noonday instant of temporal consciousness:

> Temple of Time, in a single sigh resumed,
> To this pure pitch ascending, I attune
> Myself, surrounded by a gazing sea. . . .[16]

Valéry's momentary vision of the absolute, imagistically associated with the tranquil sea and the noonday sun but flawed by human change, strongly parallels Bachelard's conception of human time as a vertical escape from materiality into the realm of thought and form. Unlike Valéry, Bachelard does not imagine the absolute along his vertical axis, but, for a self-avowed rationalist like Bachelard, (*cogito*)[3] may be the least ephemeral form of human existence, the closest man can get to the absolute.

The fullest use of reason remains Bachelard's goal, his frame of reference, even as he discovers "passages, harmonies, totally Baudelairian correspondences between pure thought and pure poetry" (*DD,* xi) through his rhythmanalytical meditation on time. Such correspondences should not surprise us when we consider that reason, for Bachelard, has all the creative power of poetry, that a "surrationalism" corresponds to the inventive flexibility of poetic "surrealism." In an article published the same year as *La Dialectique de la durée,* Bachelard proclaims that a "psychical revolution has surely just occurred in this century; human reason has just cast off, the mental voyage has begun and knowledge has left the shores of immediate reality. . . . And so a closed rationalism yields to an open rationalism."[17] With creativity as their link, reason and certain kinds of contemporary poetry (that of Valéry and the surrealists, in particular) converge in a similar reordering of immediate reality.

Alongside his growing, epistemologically inspired conviction that man has a destiny of knowledge, Bachelard's phenomenological investigation of temporal reality leads him to consider the possibility of a complementary human destiny:

Poetry might thus not be an accident, a detail, an amusement of being? It might be the very principle of creative evolution? Man might have a poetic destiny? He might be on Earth to sing the dialectic of joys and sorrows? These are a whole order of questions that we did not have the qualifications to pursue. (*DD,* xi)

Yet despite his professed limitations, Bachelard is drawn to poetry as an expression of a temporal reality. Because such poetry displays all the flexibility and independence of scientifically inspired reason, it seems able to respond to Bachelard's limited ontological quest without threatening his epistemological convictions. Indeed, as we have seen, references to scientific knowledge actually bolster Bachelard's intuitions of temporal reality. Poetry parallels the creativity of thought and suggests a value for man's aesthetic activity that is related to being rather than to knowing. This is a remarkable concession to ontology for a man who heretofore has consistently sought to reflect the light of reason. On the verge of his exploration of the elemental imagination, it is likely that, despite affinities with Valéry, Bachelard would only partially agree with the poet that

to reflect the light
Supposes a dark half always in the shadow. [18]

As Bachelard is beginning to discover, the "dark half " has a fire of its own.

Chapter Five

Fire, Water, and the Material Imagination

The title of Bachelard's 1938 essay, *The Psychoanalysis of Fire,* is both preposterous and intriguing. How can a material phenomenon like fire be "psychoanalyzed"? Is this a book of science or of fantasy? The answer, of course, is that it is a little of both, although not necessarily for reasons suggested by the title. Bachelard's initial intention is quite clearly to respond to the concerns of science, to write a book of epistemology by examining the facile assumption that objectivity results from studying objects. In *La Formation de l'esprit scientifique,* published earlier that year, he shows how such an attitude, an outgrowth of traditional philosophical realism, actually constitutes an obstacle to the rationally constructed knowledge of contemporary science. Immediate, everyday reality can elicit wonder and can cloud rational detachment. Objective knowledge must be freed from such subjective responses, it must be "psychoanalyzed." Bachelard's research for *La Formation* had shown him that among the most widespread and tenacious of such subjective images in imaginative literature were those associated with fire.[1] These vestiges of unexamined attitudes about fire represent a specific challenge for the "psychoanalysis of objective knowledge."

Poetry and Science as Complementary Opposites

Objectivity requires not only that sensations and commonsense associations with matter be critically assessed, but that words themselves be subject to the scrutiny of objective thought, "for words, which are made for singing and enchanting, rarely make contact with thought."[2] The poetry inspired by matter is dangerously seductive. Requiring caution, but awakening sensibilities, it draws forth an ambivalent response from Bachelard the epistemologist. Like fire, poetry can be both destructive and fascinating.

Beginning with the warning that "the axes of poetry and science are opposed to one another from the outset"(*PF, 2*), and setting out to catalogue the dangers of the imagination of fire for objective thought, Bachelard is gradually drawn nonetheless toward a most sympathetic treatment of the poetic power of the imagination of fire. It is a luxury he allows himself with the understanding that philosophy can only hope "to make poetry and science complementary, to unite them as two well-defined opposites" (*PF, 2*). Bachelard's self-imposed challenge is to explore the axes of poetry and of science while respecting the demands of each. Like the polarity of description and retrieval so central to his epistemology, this challenge is fundamental to all of his subsequent work. And, as was the case earlier, this twofold challenge will be met in varying ways.

Initially, Bachelard's objective in *The Psychoanalysis of Fire* does not differ appreciably from that of *La Formation de l'esprit scientifique*. He continues to seek a maximum degree of rationality and, in this case, he does so by identifying conditions under which images of fire are created. As with its Freudian model, the implied hope of Bachelard's "psychoanalysis" is that, once the subconscious, image-producing processes are exposed and understood, the rational mind will be freed from their influences. His purpose is therapeutic, as he seeks to separate scientific abstraction from the "illness" of subjectivity by resolving whether a text is meant to be understood subjectively or objectively:

This determination of the axis of explanation, whether it should be subjective or objective, appears to us to be the first diagnosis required for a psychoanalysis of knowledge. If, in a particular field of knowledge, the sum of personal convictions exceeds the sum of the items of knowledge that can be stated explicitly, taught, and proven, then a psychoanalysis is indispensable. The psychology of the scientist must tend towards a psychology that is clearly normative; the scientist must resist *personalizing his knowledge;* correlatively he must endeavor to *socialize his convictions.* (*PF,* 76–77)

Bachelard, of course, is hardly interested in developing an orthodox generalized therapy. His "psychoanalysis" is exclusively concerned with norms for a rationally based objectivity. He is Freudian only as far as it suits his purpose.

As Bachelard sees it, the threat to objective knowledge does not come so much from the depths of a repressed subconscious as from a less profound layer of commonly held semiconscious attitudes or images. Such a notion has at least as much to do with Jung's archetypes as it does with Freudian interpretation of dreams.[3] For, despite his Freudian terminology, Bachelard is less concerned with reducing images to a hidden, individual meaning than with exploring the way in which shared imaginative responses cluster around a common phenomenon like fire. For this reason, Bachelard finds semiconscious *reverie* to be more significant than subconscious *dream.* He explains that, "since we are limiting ourselves to psychoanalyzing a psychic layer that is less deep, more intellectualized, we must replace the study of dreams by the study of reverie, and, more particularly, in this little book we must study the reverie before the fire. In our opinion, this reverie is entirely different from the dream by the very fact that it is always more or less centered upon one object" (*PF,* 14). It is precisely because fire is so commonplace that the reveries associated with it may go unnoticed and thus present a surreptitious risk to the quest for objective knowledge.

While the danger for the prescientific mind was that reveries of fire usually blocked the development of objective knowledge, in the contemporary scientific era, the peril, while different, is no less real since the very attractiveness of such images can distort an existing rationalism by distracting from the rigors of rational thought. Bachelard must therefore concentrate on those very features which make images of fire attractive, those features which give reverie the power of reality. In one sense, there is nothing new in this, since he had frequently warned about the danger of relating surface qualities to an assumed, underlying substance, of treating the descriptive word as a manifestation of the substantial reality of a phenomenon. It will be recalled that such attitudes were the source of epistemological obstacles, which, in *La Formation de l'esprit scientifique,* had been associated with a prescientific philosophical realism. But we have also seen that it is not until he develops the notion of epistemological profile in *The Philosophy of No* that Bachelard makes clear his opinion that prescientific attitudes survive even in the new scientific mind. Published two years earlier, *The Psychoanalysis of Fire* already provides an indication that, with respect to the phenomenon of fire at least, "personal intuitions and scientific experiments are intermingled" (*PF,* 3).

Bachelard's readings on fire lead him to the conclusion that "the initial charm of the object is so strong that it still has the power to warp the minds of the clearest thinkers and to keep bringing them back to the poetic fold in which dreams replace thought and poems conceal theorems" (*PF,* 2). Pointing out that he had previously examined objective approaches to heat phenomena in *L'Etude de l'évolution d'un problème de physique,* Bachelard now sets out to explore "the other axis—no longer the axis of objectification but that of subjectivity" (*PF,* 3). In terms of this goal, the only significant difference from *La Formation de l'esprit scientifique* is that he now concentrates on subjective postures clustered around images of a single element. In this sense, the purpose of *The Psychoanalysis of Fire* is to illustrate further *La Formation* by focusing on a single epistemological obstacle.

Fire and Complexes

In keeping with his Freudian frame of reference, Bachelard revives his liberal use of the term "complex,"[4] which now is used to categorize the various subjective attitudes associated with fire. The tone is often anecdotal, as when Bachelard recounts his memories of having stolen matches as a boy in order to build a secret fire. "What we first learn about fire is that we must not touch it" (*PF,* 11), he recalls. The rebellion against this interdiction he names, appropriately enough, the "Prometheus complex." But, emphasizing that he is "examining a zone that is less deep than that in which primitive instincts function" (*PF,* 12), he insists on the intellectual character of the Prometheus complex. It translates the impetus *"to know* as much as our fathers, more than our fathers" so that it might suitably be called "the Oedipus complex of the life of the intellect" (*PF,* 12).

Like the Oedipus complex, the Prometheus complex represents an attitude that is fundamentally ambivalent. In a more extreme form, the reverie associated with a small, local fire is broadened to include a similarly ambivalent attitude in the face of cataclysmic fire. Expressing both fascination and terror as it moves from "the hearth to the volcano," such a reverie joins "the instinct for living and the instinct for dying" (*PF,* 16). Bachelard names this attitude the "Empedocles complex," after the fifth-century-B.C. Greek philosopher who, according to legend, died by throwing himself into the crater of Mount Etna.

But subjectivity is not only expressed as ambivalence. Bachelard invents several other complexes to identify mainly positive reveries of fire. Among them is the "Novalis complex," Bachelard's speculation on the origin of fire. Convinced that an examination of primitive *psychology* would be more revealing than what he considers to be the much weaker objective reasons usually advanced for the discovery of fire, Bachelard does not rely on anthropological studies of contemporary primitive people to explain the origins of fire. Instead, he explores the psychological attitudes of eighteenth-century nonscientists faced with a new phenomenon of fire—that of electricity. He also suggests the need for a "psychoanalytical interpretation" (*PF,* 35) of J. G. Frazer's *The Golden Bough* and *Myths of the Origin of Fire.* Bachelard attributes the early association of fire with rubbing, not to an imitation of some natural phenomenon, but to the subjective lessons of sexual experience. Similarly, he explains various customs described by Frazer by referring to their association with sexual activity rather than to their utility, so that "the explanation by the *useful* must give way to the explanation by the *agreeable,* the rational explanation must give way to the psychoanalytical explanation" (*PF,* 33).

Bachelard sees in the poetry and short stories of Novalis a similar intuition of the sexually inspired origin of fire, manifested in a "Novalis complex . . . characterized by a consciousness of inner heat which always takes precedence over a purely visual knowledge of light" (*PF*, 40). In opposing inner consciousness and visual knowledge, Bachelard attempts to account for the power of the imagination of fire by treating it on its own terms, as a subjective phenomenon. He dismisses positivistic explanations as missing the mark, for the *"objective* interpretation, while it discovers a chemical cause of the phenomenon that fills us with wonder, will never take us to the center of the image, to the kernel of the Novalis complex" (*PF*, 41). Thus Bachelard, an avowed rationalist, finds himself arguing against the role of reason!

Yet, despite this shift, he remains consistent in several respects. He had previously rejected the utilitarian prejudice of pragmatism in *La Formation de l'esprit scientifique* and, to the extent that rational explanations stem from what, in this case, is a predisposition toward realism, they are not justified in Bachelard's eyes. Notwithstanding the opposed axes of poetry and science, poetry shares an openness and freedom with science.[5] Moreover, by relying, however loosely, on the framework of psychoanalysis to justify his impressionistic approach to fire imagery, Bachelard is essentially substituting one form of scientifically inspired rationalism for another. Continuing a process begun in *La Dialectique de la durée* and expanded in *La Formation de l'esprit scientifique,* psychoanalysis replaces physics and mathematics as a guarantor of rationality in *The Psychoanalysis of Fire.*

Bachelard's longstanding opposition to naive realism and his more recent identification of animistic epistemological obstacles in *La Formation* are expressed somewhat playfully as the "Pantagruel complex." Surely no figure more aptly represents the association of fire with nourishment than Rabelais's ravenous giant. In a chapter entitled "The Chemistry of Fire: History of a False Problem," Bachelard turns away from the literary imagination of fire and examines the related reveries of alchemy and the embryonic chemistry and biology of the eighteenth century. Subject to substantialist prejudices with respect to fire, these fledgling sciences were even more vulnerable to taking literally

"the idea that fire *feeds itself* like a living creature" (*PF*, 64).
Bachelard gives several examples of such attempts to explain
combustion by recourse to the image of alimentation and by the
attribution of beneficial qualities to substances reputed to contain
heat. For the Pantagruel complex, fire may either consume or be
consumed, but in both cases it is equated with life.

While we may view such notions as naive and give them a
metaphorical interpretation, Bachelard warns us not to forget
"that they correspond to psychological realities" (*PF*, 70). In fact,
he is convinced that these realities still persist in contemporary
notions of fire. "There is still a trace of concreteness in certain
soundly abstract definitions. A psychoanalysis of objective knowledge must retrace and complete this process of *de-realization*" (*PF*,
70).

Beginning a Theory of the Literary Imagination

If we were to identify a particular moment as the one when
Bachelard finally "crosses over" from science to poetry, it would
have to be the sixth chapter of *The Psychoanalysis of Fire*, wherein
he discusses the "Hoffmann complex." The name is a reference
to the German romantic Ernst Theodor Amadeus Hoffmann,
whose tales of fantasy are largely inspired by intuitions of alcohol
or "fire-water." Here there is no longer any question of psychoanalyzing objective knowledge. Rather, Bachelard examines,
both in literature and in prescientific writings, the proposition
that "alcohol is a creator of language" (*PF*, 87). The bonhomie
and gentle irony of our "peasant" from Champagne is not lost
when he finds that reveries of alcohol and fire inspire poets and
novelists as well as writers of moralistic tracts on the "spontaneous
combustion" of alcoholics.

Bachelard seems to have discovered, in his childhood recollec-
tions of his parents preparing a burnt-brandy or *brulôt*, a sense
of the material base of the imagination. He finds in his own
reveries of fire, echoed in those of Hoffmann and others, a close
association of subject and object,[6] which leads him to propose
his now famous four-part classification of the imagination:

The precise and concrete bases must not be forgotten, if we wish to understand the psychological meaning of literary constructions. . . . If our present work serves any useful purpose, it should suggest a classification of objective themes which would prepare the way for a classification of poetic temperaments. We have not yet been able to perfect an over-all doctrine, but it seems quite clear to us that there is some relation between the doctrine of the four physical elements and the doctrine of the four temperaments. In any case, the four categories of souls in whose dreams fire, water, air, or earth predominate, show themselves to be markedly different. Fire and water, particularly, remain enemies even in reverie, and the person who listens to the sound of the stream can scarcely comprehend the person who hears the song of the flames: they do not speak the same language. (*PF,* 89)

Such a proposal is ripe for misinterpretation, especially if applied too rigidly. Indeed, Bachelard warns that he is "not dealing here with matter, but with orientation. It is not a question of being rooted in a particular substance, but of tendencies, of poetic exaltation" (*PF,* 90). What he is suggesting is that the reveries of certain writers gravitate toward images of one of the four elements and that such tendencies can be detected in their language. It is thus a question of imagination and language rather than of specific concrete reality. As Jacques Gagey points out, "the four elements, taken as names, are more the symbol of the substance than the substance itself. Earth, water, fire, and air qualify as inductors of the poetic logos and of reverie, not as a function of their objective determination, but as images."[7]

The traditional realism associated with the notion of four elements, or with any fundamental substance,[8] has long been rejected by science. And Bachelard is not reversing himself here by suggesting that such realism should now be accepted by epistemology. Rather, he continues to recognize the fundamentally subjective nature of naive realism, but he also comes to the conclusion that, while it may be a threat to scientific objectivity, it is also a source of poetry. This is tantamount to recognizing that he, and by implication any of us, can respond to the ontological temptation of beauty without abandoning the search for knowledge.

It is as if, after years of the rigorous isolation required by rationalism and the respect for objective knowledge, Bachelard has found a way to enjoy the intersubjective pleasures of poetry "legitimately," that is to say, while still maintaining the goal of objectivity. He proposes this difficult balancing act toward the end of *The Psychoanalysis of Fire,* not by liberating unconsciously repressed subjectivity, in the manner of classical psychoanalysis, but by *consciously* repressing it, so that "the error is recognized as such, but it remains as an object of good-natured polemic" (*PF,* 100). He clearly hopes that this process, which, in an echo of the dialectical transcendence of science, he calls *"dialectical sublimation"* (*PF,* 100), will both allow the image to exist and allow him to study it objectively. For, as he says, "how much more intense is this enjoyment when our objective knowledge is the objective knowledge of the *subjective,* when we discover in our own heart the human universal, when, after having honestly psychoanalyzed our study of self, we integrate the rules of morality with the laws of psychology!" (*PF,* 101).

Central to this almost puritanical approach to reverie is Bachelard's fundamental ambivalence toward the poetic imagination. Like burnt-brandy or like fire itself, imagination is something to be enjoyed, but also something to be controlled. Chastened by his epistemological background, he approaches this new psychological reality primarily as something to be known within the constraints of rationally organized knowledge. This is evinced by his recourse to the taxonomy of the elemental imagination, which he revealingly calls "this Physics or this Chemistry of reverie" (*PF,* 90). Even when, toward the end of the book, the ground shifts from reveries, which can be known psychoanalytically, to the poetic images themselves, Bachelard continues to insist that "it would be interesting to match the psychological study of reverie with the objective study of the images that entrance us" (*PF,* 107). In short, having set out to examine reveries specifically associated with fire in order further to psychoanalyze objective knowledge, to free it from the influence of reverie, Bachelard is led to the discovery of the poetic expression of that reverie, to the particular verbal images produced by the imagination of fire.

This discovery prompts a call for "an objective literary criticism" (*PF*, 109), which would continue the objective study of reverie he has begun. But, although he may sound particularly modern when he suggests that "a poetic mind is purely and simply a syntax of metaphors" (*PF*, 109), he warns that any attempt at criticism "must find the way to integrate the hesitations, the ambiguities" (*PF*, 110) that precede the poem itself and are part of the creative process. For Bachelard, the imagination is "an autochtonous, autogenous realm . . . the true source of psychic production" (*PF*, 110), and, ultimately, it cannot be determined by objective means. It is a measure of Bachelard's ambivalence vis-à-vis the imagination that what began as an attempt to understand imaginative processes objectively should end with a cautionary reminder of the irredeemable subjectivity of the imagination. It is also a measure of that ambivalence that, despite his recognition of this indeterminable subjectivity, he should continue to imitate the taxonomic approach of early science in the works that follow.

Lautréamont and the Lessons of Science and Poetry

Before Bachelard turns his attention again to the elemental imagination, he undertakes, with *Lautréamont* (1939), his only extended examination of a single author's work, that of "The Count of Lautréamont," penname for the nineteenth-century poet Isidore Ducasse. This study of Lautréamont's *Les Chants de Maldoror* allows Bachelard to explore more fully some of the implications of the *Psychoanalysis of Fire* for the literary imagination and to concentrate on a literary work, as such, rather than to use literary images as illustrations for an essay on objective knowledge.

He continues to place value on the goal of unfettered thought in *Lautréamont*, where a *"Psychoanalysis of Life"*[9] follows his earlier *Psychoanalysis of Fire*, but, in choosing a particularly unconventional work as the subject of his study, Bachelard also associates this freedom with the imagination. Throughout *Lautréamont* Bachelard's critical stance is informed by two main perspectives: the practice of contemporary science and his more recent tendency to reduce an imaginative text to one or two categories of images.

Thus *Lautréamont* summarizes Bachelard's dilemma with respect to imaginative literature: for much of his subsequent writing on the literary imagination, he will be torn between preserving the essentially epistemological perspective of science, with its emphasis on method, or acquiescing in the ontological outlook of imaginative literature, with its emphasis on symbolic reality.

As Bachelard sees it, Lautréamont's work inaugurates a *"primitive* poetry which must create its language" (*L,* 53), a language of energetic, animalistic imagery, which can be reduced to two basic images of animal aggression: clawing and suction. With its brutal imagery, this new language replaces the space-conscious *form* of descriptive poetry with the time-conscious *function* of a new, dynamic poetry. In *Les Chants de Maldoror,* action replaces fixed rational classifications as "the function creates the organ" (*L,* 24). By contrast, notes Bachelard, the animal imagery of a poet like Leconte de Lisle is static and overly visual. It betrays the influence of a formal and rational tradition, while Lautréamont's aggressive imagery is a willful attack on the dogmatic past. Here Bachelard sees in Lautréamont's exaggerated dynamism an adolescent rebellion against books and teachers, an energetic espousal of life against the irrationalism of imposed authority. Grounded in the specific sociocultural situation of the adolescent in nineteenth-century France, such a rebellion promotes *"cultural complexes"* (*L,* 62) of fear and cruelty which must find their resolution within the culture itself, which is to say, in literature. Thus, for the first time, Bachelard is brought to a sustained study of the literary imagination as such.

Lautréamont's literary resolution to his cultural complexes is to forge what Bachelard calls, in imitation of projective geometry, a *"projective poetry"* (*L,* 54) in which certain images are projected beyond the usual limits of poetic form, while still displaying an underlying poetic coherence within a particular group of images. Here, then, Bachelard combines the lessons of a transcendent, or projective, science with the ontological reduction to fundamental images inspired by psychoanalysis; Lautréamont's clusters of images are not only projective, they also appear to be obsessive. Nevertheless Bachelard defends Lautréamont against the charge that these clusters of images reveal the obsessions of a madman by referring to Gide's definition of man as " 'the animal capable of a gratuitous action' " (*L*, 138). He points to the variety of imagery, to the many metamorphoses of *Les Chants de Maldoror* as evidence that Lautréamont escaped from the determinism of animal instinct, from the monomania of madness.

Despite its aggressive animal imagery, Bachelard maintains that Lautréamont's poetry is a human poetry, a pioneering work that creates by violating reality. Yet it is limited by its heavy reliance on what Bachelard calls "the efficient causality of natural gestures" (*L*, 153), by a certain lack of control inherent in the use of such forceful animal imagery. Now that Lautréamont has freed poetry from the yoke of description, what is needed, concludes Bachelard, is "a kind of *non-Lautréamontism* which must, in every way, go beyond *Les Chants de Maldoror*" (*L*, 154). Using the term in the same way as non-Euclidism, Bachelard seeks a conversion of Lautréamont's work which, like transcendent science and mathematics, will not oppose Lautréamont's metamorphoses but will realize their potential by integrating them into a more fully human poetry. Poetry, like thought, must resist immediate reality: "For us the choice is made: new thought and new poetry require a break and a conversion. . . . No value is specifically human if it is not the result of a renunciation and a conversion. A specifically human value is always a *converted* natural value. Lautréamontism, the result of a first dynamization, thus seems a value to be converted, a force of expansion to be transformed" (*L*, 155–56).

The lesson has consequences for Bachelard's own approach to literature. In treating the work of this most original poet, he perceives the possibility of converting the values of science, especially nondeterminism and dialectical transcendence, to human cultural values, including literature in particular. Bachelard's thorough familiarity with the revolutionary nature of contemporary science clearly enables him to understand the power, the significance, and even the limits of Lautréamont's poetry. For, once Bachelard's disclosures on the "Copernican revolution" in modern science are understood, once it is clear that the fundamental lesson of contemporary science is the need to reject the rigid determinism or a priori outlooks, there is no enigma in the fact that an epistemologist can come to such a sympathetic understanding of a work that initially seems so profoundly irrational. Lautréamont's poetry allows Bachelard to confirm that, if the axes of poetry and science are initially opposed, they nevertheless can share a common spirit. As Vincent Therrien suggests in his monumental *Révolution de Gaston Bachelard en critique littéraire*, there is in Bachelard a "new literary mind" which corresponds to his "new scientific mind"[10] and its first full expression is to be found in *Lautréamont*.

Water and Cultural Complexes

In a frequently quoted passage from *L'Eau et les rêves* (1942), Bachelard proclaims his continuing goal of becoming a rationalist while acknowledging his failure to do so when it comes to images of water:

A rationalist? We are attempting to *become* one, not only in the whole of our culture, but in the detail of our thoughts, in the detailed order of our familiar images. And it is in this way, by a psychoanalysis of objective knowledge and of image-laden knowledge, that we have become a rationalist with respect to fire. Sincerity requires us to confess that we have not achieved a similar reform when it comes to water. We are still living images of water, we live them synthetically, in their initial complexity, by giving them often our unreasoned adherence.[11]

This does not mean that his analysis of such images is unreasoned, however.[12] But it does indicate that the role of psychoanalysis will be greatly reduced. "To speak of psychoanalysis, it is necessary to have classified the original images without allowing a trace of their initial privileges to remain" (*ER*, 9).

Here the vestiges of the image's privileges do remain. Rather than attempting to exorcise them as part of a "psychoanalysis of objective knowledge," Bachelard develops the conditions for a rational approach to their manifestation in language. Instead of concentrating on the sources of images as would psychoanalysis,

Bachelard focuses on the transformation of such sources when an image is put into words. He examines the circumstances surrounding the literary expression of images in an attempt to "provide a contribution to the psychology of literary creation" (*ER*, 216). The distinction here between psychology and psychoanalysis is significant. The psychology of literary creation tries to establish the connection between deep complexes born of repression and certain *"unthinking attitudes* that control the very exercise of thought" (*ER*, 25). Bachelard calls these attitudes "cultural complexes [which] are grafted onto the deeper complexes that were brought to light by psychoanalysis" (*ER*, 26). As was the case in *Lautréamont,* it is not nature but culture that he wishes to explore, although he insists that the two are linked, that like the "natural" complex of psychoanalysis, the "cultural" complex of his psychology of literary creation is a means of transforming psychic energy.

What he proposes, then, is a psychological literary criticism: "Under these conditions, a literary criticism that does not want to be limited to a static statement of images must be matched by a psychological criticism which relives the dynamic character of the imagination by following the link between original complexes and cultural complexes" (*ER*, 26). The study of cultural complexes is meant to provide a method of understanding how the imagination produces certain kinds of images. This, in turn, fits well with Bachelard's conviction that images are reducible, that they betray one of the four types of imaginations.

Less of a practitioner than an illustrator of psychological criticism, Bachelard first examines images of pure water and clear, reflecting surfaces which he associates with a *"cosmic narcissism"* (*ER*, 36–37). Such images are essentially visual; they create a serene world of surface contemplation. But it is in the tactile *"heavy water"* (*ER*, 64) of Edgar Allan Poe that the real power of the imagination of water is revealed. Here a viscous water, sometimes dark, sometimes milky, transmits a preoccupation with death and a cultural transformation of certain Oedipal impulses later studied by Marie Bonaparte.[13] This opaque water of depths rather than surfaces is, in effect, the imagined water discussed in most of *L'Eau et les rêves*; cultural complexes are invoked to express attitudes associated with what can only be described as hydrophobia.

Bachelard concludes that visual water images merely reproduce perception, that they are too conceptual, while language has the power to produce the very sound of water and thus to evoke the subjective depths of this element. When the imagination of water is truly creative, when it is not merely imitative, he insists that it is expressed verbally rather than visually, that "the real domain in which to study the imagination is not painting, it is the literary work, the word, the sentence" (*ER*, 252). Yet, despite appearances, Bachelard's quarrel is not with painting itself but with excessively conceptual *representation* as opposed to truly creative, subjective *anticipation*. For Bachelard, the poetic imagination should be inventive and such inventiveness is necessarily verbal.

As is the case in science, creativity and discovery are not found in the merely visual, in the surface reality. For the arts, too, the visual is the realm of the inauthentic, whether the medium is painting or literature. Not only are there several examples of unduly visual and aridly imitative literary images in *L'Eau et les rêves*, but, in several separately published essays on the "visual" arts, ranging from etching to painting, Bachelard associates the creative power of reverie with words.[14] While he never develops even the outlines of a linguistic theory, his predilection for language over form rests on his association of words with archetypes of the imagination and of the visual with naively rational concepts.

The Material Imagination and Reverie

In *L'Eau et les rêves* the preference for words over form is translated into a fundamental opposition between the formal and the material imagination. Recognizing that these two types of imagination are never completely separable, Bachelard nevertheless gives particular emphasis to the material imagination when he maintains that, "beyond the images of form, so often evoked by psychologists of the imagination, there are—we will show—images of matter, *direct* images of *matter*. Sight names them, but the hand knows them. A dynamic joy handles them, kneads them, lightens them. These images of matter are dreamed in their substance, intimately, by setting aside forms, perishable forms, vain images, the development of surfaces" (*ER,* 2). In the realm of the imagination, the element and not merely the object is the source of original images. Matter, which Bachelard calls the *"unconsciousness of form"* (*ER,* 70), is the hidden impulse that gives a particular image its poetic power. The object of perception is quite literally superficial, that is, it exists only as a surface and is secondary to the imagination of matter. Thus the classification of the imagination according to the four elements now becomes a four-part classification of the *material* imagination.

The fact is, of course, that despite an aversion to immediate surface reality which they share with science, many of the reveries of the material imagination, as had been the case earlier with reveries of fire, are the very epistemological obstacles that Bachelard had tried to eliminate on the way to a rationally constructed knowledge. For both prescientific philosophy and for the contemporary imagination, the fundamental importance of matter over form betrays a naive realism in which the qualities of objects are merely reflections of an underlying substance. How like Bachelard's description of philosophical realism is his observation that, with water, "color matters little; it only yields an adjective; it only designates a variety. The material imagination goes immediately to the substantial quality" (*ER,* 158). An object's color, like its shape, is a function of its appearance. These external qualities serve to *describe* the object, while the material imagination relates the object to prior reverie in which images of the underlying substance prevail. "For, in the literary order, everything is dreamed before being seen, be it the simplest of descriptions" (*ER,* 185). Description belongs to science and reverie to poetry.

Where the alchemists and scholars of prescientific eras produced a pseudoscience because this description stemmed more from prior subjective reverie than from rational construction, their contemporary heirs, the poets, create an authentic literature precisely because they are in touch with these very reveries. The apparently " 'natural learning' [of prescientific thinkers] involves 'natural'

reveries. Those are the reveries that a psychologist of the imagination must recover" (*ER,* 184–85). Unlike rationalism, which
is perfectible, and which the scientist must struggle to maintain,
reverie, for Bachelard, is a human constant that takes place naturally. We do not labor to become daydreamers, we give in to
daydreams. And while today's reveries may be about new objects
and new forms, the elemental substratum remains unchanged.

This link between prescientific realism and present-day reverie
explains why Bachelard is increasingly at pains to differentiate
between the metaphor and the image. "The prescientific mind
conceives concretely of images that we take as simple metaphors.
It really thinks that the earth *drinks* water" (*ER,* 168). The
metaphor, in Bachelard's view, merely reproduces the object of
perception. It is a visual, intellectualized figure that may even
be used to illustrate scientific concepts. The image, on the other
hand, precedes concepts; it is not limited by rational knowledge.

As an example of the image, Bachelard recalls Poe's description
of Antarctic waters in *The Narrative of Arthur Gordon Pym:* "The
heat of the water was now truly remarkable, and its color was
undergoing a rapid change, being no longer transparent, but of
a milky consistency and hue."[15] Despite the fact that it is polar
water and that, in empirical and rational terms, it ought to be
cold, Bachelard notes that we are dealing "with water as matter,
as a substance which is warm and white. It is white because it
is warm. Its heat was noticed before its whiteness" (*ER,* 166).
For, with the image, the material takes precedence over the visual,
the substantial over the rationally empirical. The result of a direct
apprehension of immediate reality through the prism of prior
reverie, the image expresses an ontological rather than an epistemological view of the world. It is this view that the poet
continues and to which Bachelard returns when he examines the
psychology of the literary imagination.

The peculiar attribute of the literary imagination is that, unlike
objective knowledge, which must be rationally constructed, it
approaches the world naively, in its concrete immediacy. In those
instances where the imagination attempts to rely on reason rather
than reverie, as when cultural complexes lose contact with deeper

psychological complexes, images are artificial, they grow out of "a naively rationalized tradition" (*ER*, 58). Such a tradition is neither good reverie, which must be "natural" and spontaneous, nor good rationality, which, in the service of contemporary science, has learned to transcend immediacy. As Bachelard points out, "we don't see any solidity to a natural, immediate, elementary rationality" (*ER*, 9–10). Immediate, concrete, naive realism, on the other hand, is the stuff of reverie. While Bachelard had discarded both naive realism and monolithic rationalism in favor of a constructed, less naive rationalism in his epistemology, he now embraces naive realism, but still rejects naive rationalism. In this way, without doing violence to the rationalistic principles of his epistemology, which he continues to uphold, he is able to recognize a new ontological perspective in "*the real phantom of our imaginary nature,* which, if it dominated our lives, would give us back the truth of our being" (*ER*, 249).

After the escape from subjectivity necessary for rational knowledge, the imagination has the therapeutic value of leading us back to what is particularly human within ourselves. "Real life is healthier if it is given its deserved vacation of irreality" (*ER*, 35). The paradox that the well-being of reality should depend on irreality is basic to Bachelard's developing ontology. It reflects his coming to terms with the notion that the reality of life, which is both objective and subjective, simply does not always follow determinable logical patterns. The literary imagination verbally expresses reverie, that inventive, unpredictable aspect of "real life." It makes of life a particularly human reality which is as nondeterministic as the reality of contemporary science.

Reverie, therefore, serves an ontological function by translating concrete, immediate reality into human terms. It is to real life what scientific reason is to the physical world. Both scientific reason and reverie transcend immediate reality. Reason does so in the direction of a constructed, objective reality, inseparable from the method of knowing, while reverie operates in the direction of a subjective reality, inseparable from its means of expression. Thus, where ontology is a function of epistemology in science—where what is known depends on how it is known—

in poetry—where what is known depends on how it is written—
it is a function of language, a "symbolic ontology."[16]

In *L'Eau et les rêves* Bachelard's focus has shifted from a primary
concern with how reality is known to a direct emphasis on a new,
particularly human reality in which the literary imagination
rather than the means of knowing plays the most fundamental
role. The "superhuman faculty" (*ER*, 23), as Bachelard calls the
imagination, is the means by which man can create an open
superreality. As Mary Ann Caws has indicated, there is, in Bachelard, a parallel between his transcendent rationalism or "surrationalism" and this new "surrealism."[17] As Bachelard's
epistemological concerns give way to ontological considerations
in the works on the four elements, or the *Elements,* as we shall
call them here, nondeterministic, transcendent openness remains
a constant human trait.

It is precisely because the imagination is a manifestation of
human openness and inventiveness that it is never content merely
to copy reality. Imagination must act upon material reality in
order to translate it into a particularly human surreality. There
is what Bachelard calls a *"coefficient of adversity"* (*ER,* 213) between
the imagination and reality. Reverie, the means by which imagination transforms reality into human terms, is therefore not
neutral. In confronting reality it must conquer an adversary that
resists. Its transformations of reality are victories similar to those
of objective knowledge when it tries to understand reality.

Such victories of the imagination over reality may take various
forms, but, in the case of water, Bachelard identifies two major
types of triumph that have found verbal expression. The first,
which he calls the "Swinburne complex," after the nineteenth-
century English poet Algernon Charles Swinburne, expresses the
ambivalence of the swimmer who initially is sadistically victorious
over water but who ultimately is defeated by that element. "Fa-
tigue is the fate of the swimmer: sadism must give way, sooner
or later, to masochism" (*ER,* 227). But Bachelard also detects
"a more clearly sadistic complex" (*ER,* 241), which he names the
"Xerxes complex," after the Persian king who, according to
Herodotus, ordered the Hellespont whipped when a storm de-

stroyed the bridges he had built. Both complexes recognize that the imagination assigns a value (either negative or positive, and occasionally both) to an element such as water.

This valorization also takes place when a quality, such as purity or impurity, is recognized imaginatively in water. As happens in traditional philosophical realism, all such qualities are attributed to the element itself, to the substance which, in terms of the imagination, acts either purely or impurely. For the imagination, even a small amount of pure water can purify a far greater amount, while the reverse is also true of a small quantity of impure water. Bachelard calls this action of valorized substance "a fundamental law of the *material imagination*" (*ER*, 194).[18] When the imagination assigns value to a substance, it also assigns it the will to act. This animism marks "a transformation from the material imagination to the dynamic imagination" (*ER*, 195), of which the Swinburne complex and the Xerxes complex are two examples. Just as animism was related to substantialism in prescientific times, the dynamic imagination grows out of and is linked to the material imagination and both are opposed to the more superficial formal imagination. But a more complete consideration of the dynamic imagination shall await Bachelard's exploration of the imagination of air and earth.

The Question of Method

In any discussion of Bachelard's first two books on the elemental imagination, it is easy to overlook his many methodological hesitations. As he moves from the *Psychoanalysis of Fire* to *L'Eau et les rêves,* he clearly has discovered in the literary imagination a worthy object of study. This is new ground, a new axis, with echoes of prescientific, naive realism, although its very source— reverie—parallels the nondeterministic constructive reason of science. While Bachelard appears to recognize the intricacy of his discovery, he still seems uncertain as to the best approach to take in exploring it. The reader is left with a sense that Bachelard is stumbling toward a method, that some of his proposals, including his categorization according to the four elements and his differentiation among the formal, the material, and the dynamic imaginations may well be the results of sudden inspiration and that they have yet to be incorporated into a carefully worked out theory. At the same time, the literary imagination legitimizes naive realism thereby making previously limited ontological considerations a central concern for the first time in Bachelard's work.

Neither the primary focus on ontology nor the serendipitous approach to concepts is typical of most of Bachelard's prior work, so that it seems likely that both the overall reference to psycho-analysis and psychology and the preservation of his categories of the imagination are means by which to continue his investigation of the literary image without having actually to confront the question of method, and without having to relinquish his fundamental confidence in science and reason. Yet all such borrowings are applied loosely; they are adapted to the particularities of the literary imagination with a flexibility that is both worthy of and undoubtedly inspired by his philosophy of science. Nevertheless, as he completes his first two books on the elemental imagination, the means of knowing has ebbed as his single major concern. Finding himself somewhere between the psychology of symbolization and literary criticism, Bachelard turns his attention increasingly to how images are produced and expressed, with only a passing glance at the appropriateness of his approach.

Chapter Six

Air, Earth, and the Dynamic Imagination

Air and Dynamic Vertical Imagery

In *L'Air et les songes* (1943), his third book on the elements, Bachelard pursues his psychology of the literary imagination, although allusions to "complexes" have now virtually been replaced by accounts of "sublimation," more in keeping with what he views as the vertical axis of the aerial imagination. Divided almost evenly between a consideration of general dreams of flying, of falling, and of height and images of specific physical phenomena such as sky, stellar space, and wind, the book even includes a chapter on the tree, whose verticality and stature associate it with air. Non-French writers like Milton, Shelley, Rilke, Nietzsche, Novalis, and D'Annunzio join Balzac, Nodier, Supervielle, Éluard, Milọsz,[1] and others in providing examples of the aerial imagination. This greatly expanded list of authors reflects an increased preoccupation with the specifically literary aspect of the psychology of the imagination.

Bachelard continues to focus on questions of ontology and literary criticism, two concerns which his previous books on the elemental imagination had only begun to develop. Yet, while he deals much more extensively with these difficult issues in *L'Air et les songes,* he does not seem to have resolved them to his satisfaction. Thus he must write two conclusions—one on the literary image, the other on the philosophy of motion—with only a very brief, though suggestive, final attempt to find common ground for both literature and metaphysics.

The dual conclusions of *L'Air et les songes* are themselves a result of the two principal goals which Bachelard proposes for this study. Convinced that the poetic imagination is not static, that to imagine is not to perceive but to sally forth toward a new world and to leave ordinary reality behind, Bachelard likens imagination to a Baudelairian *"invitation au voyage."*[2] As his subtitle indicates, this is an *Essay on the Imagination of Motion* and his first objective is to attempt to follow the movement of the imagination, to trace the "journey from the real to the imaginary" (*AS,* 11). This journey will vary according to the element of the poet's inspiration, but, in Bachelard's view, air is particularly well suited to conveying the notion that "the means by which we escape from the real clearly designates our innermost reality" (*AS,* 14). In other words, air, with its dynamism and immateriality, does not evoke a prescientific ontology based on naive realism, as does water, but allows instead for the full expression of *subjective* reality. The ontological dimension is still present but, in keeping with the way the imagination functions, the inner "reality" in question can only be revealed by a movement toward an imagined irreality. Bachelard's intention is to examine the dynamic continuity from the real to the imaginary which will allow the inner reality to be known.[3]

The second goal is more implicit, although, as sometimes happens with Bachelard, it is ultimately revealed toward the end of his study. In this case, in a transitional paragraph, just before the final chapter on "The Mute Word," Bachelard reminds his reader not only that he is focusing on the imagination of air but that "we want to limit ourselves to a study of the *literary* metaphors of air" (*AS,* 270, emphasis added). As he explains in the succeeding chapter, poetry grows out of a will to speak, and it is in this *"will to logos"* (*AS,* 278), as he calls it, that the imagination is at work. To study the continuum of the imagination as it moves from reality to irreality must, therefore, require that we also study the verbal expression that makes such a movement possible.

And what of the psychology of the literary imagination? While its role is reduced, it nevertheless continues to provide a flexible frame of reference for Bachelard's dual pursuits. Thus, speaking of his first goal, Bachelard declares his intention unhesitatingly to use "psychological observations as a pretext for developing [his] own theses on the metaphysics of the imagination" (*AS,* 24). His second aim of examining specifically literary images as manifestations of the will to logos has much to do with his many references to "sublimation," a term Bachelard borrows from psychology to "explain" the upward motion of most aerial images. But perhaps the most appropriate indication of the flexibility with which he applies the psychological framework both to the imagination and to the will to logos is to be found in the title itself, where *songes* has replaced the more straightforward *rêves.* Both *rêve* and *songe* would be translated as "dream," but the verb form, *songer,* carries notions of will and thought not associated with *rêver.* In speaking of *L'Air et les songes* rather than *L'Air et les rêves,* Bachelard is able to draw on these connotations to suggest the new ways in which he is now looking at the imagination.

The element of air seems hardly suited for a consideration of the material imagination, "for air is meager matter" (*AS,* 15). With writers inspired by the aerial imagination, the material imagination is one of sublimation in the physical as well as the psychological sense: in the imagination of air solid matter is lost, as when a substance "sublimates" into a gas. As Bachelard indicates, "the substantial imagination of air is truly active only in a dynamic of dematerialization" (*AS,* 188). Thus, even when viewed from the perspective of the material imagination, air is a mobile element. Because it is ethereal it can inspire the poetic imagination only through its dynamism, although, as is the case with the sublimation of a substance, this dynamism must have a material base. Air inspires the imagination of motion, but it also requires the imagination of matter at its source. It provides ample justification for stressing the dynamic imagination, but it also allows Bachelard to maintain the categories of the imagination of elements set up in *The Psychoanalysis of Fire.* The "theoretical" framework is thus preserved, although this may be due more to Bachelard's sensitivity in adapting to the peculiarities of highly original writers and his use of convenient examples from lesser writers rather than to the adequacy of his theory, as such.[4] This would explain why uninspired attempts to apply Bachelard's quaternary "law" of the imagination as an inflexible method of literary criticism seem destined to fail.[5]

When we consider physical sublimation as the model for the dynamic dematerialization of air, it is not surprising that the aerial imagination should inspire images of ascension. Bachelard calls such images *"axiomatic* [since] nothing explains them and they explain everything" (*AS,* 18). At issue here is the primacy of the imagination over reason, first suggested in *The Psychoanalysis of Fire* with respect to the question of the origin of fire. Just as he had rejected rationalistic explanations attributing the discovery of fire to pragmatic concerns, Bachelard argues against attempts to explain conceptually dreams of flying.

It might seem reasonable to assume, for example, that a person having dreams of flight imagines himself to have wings. Yet the literary passages which Bachelard examines (particularly those of Nodier, Rilke, and Shelley) demonstrate that, in the imagination, the act of flying has no need of wings. A result of the formal imagination, *"the wing is already a rationalization,"* while a truly *"oneiric flight is never a winged flight"* (*AS,* 36). There are, of course, images of winged flight (Icarus, for example), but, as Bachelard sees it, such images are poetically inauthentic because they are not faithful to their original oneiric inspiration. "Henceforth, in our view, *when a wing appears in the account of a dream of flight, a rationalization of this account must be suspected.* One can be fairly certain that the account is contaminated, either by images of awakened thought or by bookish inspirations" (*AS,* 36). The preference here is for the material imagination of flight over the formal imagination of wings. For Bachelard, it is a basic "principle that in the world of dream one does not fly because one has wings, one believes one has wings because one has flown" (*AS,* 36).

Because the dynamic imagination inspired by air is essentially an upward motion, it readily translates the aspirations of human will. Its function is not only literary but psychoanalytical, as Bachelard discovers in the work of Robert Desoille. The therapeutic methods of this Swiss psychiatrist are designed to induce dreams of ascension in order to encourage the process of sublimation and free the blocked psyche.[6] It is a question, ultimately, of "matching one's life to one's imagination" (*AS,* 130); the dynamic imagination has therapeutic value because it frees the inner being. The counterpart to this position, of course, is that images of falling indicate psychological repression; they represent an abnormal direction for the dynamic imagination. "We will therefore study the imagination of the fall as a kind of illness of the imagination of ascent, as an *inexplicable nostalgia* for height" (*AS,* 111). The direction in which the aerial imagination moves along this axis gives it a positive or negative value. Thus the dynamic imagination associated with air is never morally neutral. Where Desoille makes use of the principle that "all valorization is verticalization" (*AS,* 18) in his therapy, Bachelard applies the same notion to literature and, beyond that, to metaphysics. Because the "imagination is necessarily a valorization" (*AS,* 296) when it moves along a vertical axis, it cannot escape the destiny that its dynamism imposes.

Bachelard is very careful not to suggest that images of falling are of less aesthetic value than images of ascent. On the contrary, the greater the beauty of any image, the greater its power to disclose either a positive or negative moral value. But the valorization that results from images of rising and falling does have ontological consequences since it serves to reveal a subjective reality. "For a fully dynamic aerial imagination, everything that *rises* is awakened to being, participates in being. Conversely, everything that is lowered is dispersed into vain shadows and partakes of nothingness. *Valorization determines being:* that is one of the great principles of imagination" (*AS,* 90). In the dynamic imagination beauty is primary; it reveals value. Thus Bachelard's metaphysical thesis and Desoille's psychological theory are mutually supportive when it is understood that a positive value results from images of ascent and designates both being and well-being, while a negative value is the consequence of images of falling and indicates both a reduction of being and illness.

But it bears repeating that a basic principle of this entire doctrine is the primacy of the imagination. The power of its imagery not only reveals the vertical axis from reduced being to full being (or from illness to well-being), but it is precisely that imagery that makes it possible to *attain* the fullest being and the greatest well-being. Influenced by French psychiatrist Pierre Janet's concept of *reality function,* Freud had stressed the importance of the reality principle for psychological well-being,[7] but Bachelard insists on the fundamental importance of the *unreality function* when he claims that "a person deprived of the *unreality function* is as much of a neurotic as a person deprived of the *reality function*" (*AS,* 14). In short, imagination is essential to the fullest flowering of the *human* being.

The Copernican Revolution of the Imagination

Imagination and image are closely linked. The first is the subjective, dynamic process by which reality is transformed, by which the psyche frees itself from reality. The second is the verbal means through which that conversion takes place. Together they transform not only external reality but inner, subjective reality as well. From an external, objective point of view, both the imagination and the image are unreal, yet because both serve to determine inner being they have a subjective reality and a subjective function. Bachelard cautions against considering the image merely as the product of the imagination: "At its birth, in its flight, the image is, within us, the subject of the verb to imagine. It is not its object" (*AS,* 22). We imagine because of the image, we do not produce an image because we imagine.

But this close association of image and imagination as partners in the transformation of reality can lead to some ontological confusion. We find Bachelard variously claiming that "images are the first psychic realities" (*AS,* 297), or that "imagination is being itself, a being yielding its images and its thoughts" (*AS,* 127). We are confronted here, once again, with evidence that Bachelard's *Elements* have only the trappings of a theory of the imagination. His earlier epistemology amply demonstrates his ability to deal cogently with abstractions. If he is to be forgiven such inconsistencies now, it must be with the understanding that all of the *Elements*, and not just *The Psychoanalysis of Fire,* represent a transition from science to poetry during which his borrowings from psychology serve as a pseudoscientific framework for his exploration of the imagination.

Bachelard's underlying ontological argument that subjective being is determined by the dynamic imagination should not be lost in the secondary debate over whether it is the image or the imagination that is most fundamental. Each is essential to the other, but, more importantly, his basic position remains consistent with his comments on reverie in *L'Eau et les rêves* that the subjective state, whether it is called reverie, dream, or imagination, precedes our perception of reality. In *L'Air et les songes* he continues to insist on this primacy of dream:

Dream is not a product of awakened life. It is the fundamental subjective state. A metaphysician will be able to see in action here a *kind of Copernican revolution of the imagination.* Indeed, images are not explained by their objective TRAITS, but by their *subjective* SENSE. This revolution amounts to placing:

> the dream before the reality,
> the nightmare before the drama,
> the terror before the monster,
> nausea before the fall;

in short, the imagination is, within the subject, alive enough to impose its visions, its dread, its misfortune. (*AS,* 119)

This "Copernican revolution" must surely recall the Copernican revolution of abstraction discussed in Chapter 3. The similarity is not merely verbal, for, in both science and poetry, Bachelard proposes a revolutionary way of looking at the relationship between mind and object or between inner being and outer reality. In both cases it is the spirit, whether reason or the imagination, that determines how external reality is perceived. The difference is that the determining factor for science is how we know, while for poetry it is who we are. The axes of science and poetry are as opposed (and as complementary) as epistemology and ontology.

But, in keeping with the second major goal of his book, the Copernican revolution of the imagination involves not only a redefinition of the relationship of subject and object, but of the correlation of the act of writing to reality; it is not only a question of who we are, but of what is written. "There is no *poetry* preceding the act of the poetic word. There is no reality preceding the literary image" (*AS,* 283). In Bachelard's view, therefore, not only is the subjective state primordial, it is necessarily verbal. The apparent confusion between imagination and literary image is the result of the essential relationship between the two: the imagination must take a linguistic form and the literary image is the self-aware recognition of that necessity. "Imagination, within us, speaks, our dreams speak, our thoughts speak. All human activity wishes to speak. When this spoken word becomes conscious of itself, then human activity wishes to write, that is to arrange dreams and thoughts. The imagination is spellbound by the literary image. Literature is not, therefore, the substitute for any other activity. It completes a human desire. It represents an *emergence* of the imagination" (*AS,* 283–84). In short, the language of literature is essential to the dynamism of the imagination; it is part of that very dynamism.

Consequently, Bachelard views as "unjust, a criticism that sees in language only a hardening of intimate experience" (*AS,* 288). It is precisely this sort of traditional criticism, with its emphasis on the formal imagination, that misunderstands much of contemporary literature. Bachelard's objection to a premature rationalization of the literary phenomenon based on a "utilitarian and rational education" (*AS,* 145) is not without echoes of a similar objection in science. Literature, particularly contemporary literature, requires an open-ended criticism that takes its lessons from literature itself, just as science requires an open-ended rationalism that follows the practice of contemporary science. Bachelard does not argue against conceptual criticism, but he does insist that the critic first take into account the processes of the imagination, of verbal reverie, before beginning any conceptual inquiry.

Yet comments on literary criticism are only of passing concern in *L'Air et les songes;* they are the consequence of Bachelard's preoccupation with the *"will to logos,"* with the creation of the literary image as a fundamental and universal human activity. A revised literary criticism would recognize the essential linguistic dynamism of this "very specifically human will" (*AS,* 278). What is central is not literary criticism but literature itself, or, more precisely, the art of writing, of creating literary images. It is this act that offers Bachelard the hope of reconciling the view of the imagination as a determinant of being and as a transformer of language:

As a matter of fact, the recently formed literary image adapts to the preceding language, is inscribed like a new crystal in the soil of language, but beforehand, at the moment of its formation, the literary image has met needs of expansion, of exuberance, of expression. And the two developments are linked, for it seems that to express the ineffable, the evasive, the aerial, any writer must develop themes of inner riches, of riches that have the weight of inner certainties. From then on, the literary image appears in two perspectives: the perspective of expansion and the perspective of intimacy. . . . Expansion and depth, at the moment when being discovers itself with exuberance, are dynamically linked. They induce each other. Lived in the sincerity of its images, the exuberance of being reveals its depth. Reciprocally, it seems that the depth of inner being is like an expansion with regard to itself. (*AS,* 301–302)

Through literature, and more particularly through poetry, Bachelard discovers that being cannot be limited to external reality, to that which can be conceptually designated.[8] While it is imaginative and therefore subjective, literature is not an isolated activity because it is simultaneously verbal. It is the paradigmatic or vertical axis of the aerial imagination, coupled with the syntagmatic or horizontal transformation of language that leads Bachelard to discover in literature a subjective yet communicable reality.

Earth and Aggression: A Conciliation of the Material and Dynamic Imaginations

The first of two books on the element of earth, *La Terre et les rêveries de la volonté* (1948) continues to deal with the dynamic imagination. But in a preface entitled "The Material Imagination and the Spoken Imagination," designed to apply to both "earth" books, Bachelard suggests a synthesis of the dynamic and the material imaginations. It will be recalled that the *dynamic* imagination of violent water and of air is a function of human *will;* by its imagined actions on or within the element, it reveals inner being. The *material* imagination, previously associated with water, on the other hand, reaccredits naive realism; that is, it assigns subjective values to hidden *substance.* Bachelard calls the willful, dynamic imagination extroverted, while the inward-looking material imagination, to be studied in the second book—*La Terre et les rêveries de repos*—is labeled introverted.

Yet he cautions against making too sharp a distinction between introverted and extroverted reveries, not only because they are rarely found in isolation, but because "all images are developed between the two poles, they experience dialectically the enticements of the universe and the certainties of intimacy. . . . The most beautiful images are often the sources of ambivalence."[9] For, while it may be a useful taxonomic device to classify images according to whether they move outwardly toward the world or associate the world with inner subjectivity, in both cases the imagination precedes the division of subject and object because its capacity to formulate images preexists thought and perception. The imagination's ambivalence means that "the image has a double reality: a psychic reality and a physical reality. It is through the image that the imagining being and the imagined being are closest" (*TRV,* 5). Yet both beings are imaginary; the dialectic of imaginative introversion and willful extroversion is inescapably subjective. That, and not its objective correlative, is the image's reality and the source of any synthesis of the material and dynamic imaginations.

As before, Bachelard chooses to concentrate on literary images in particular because he demurely considers himself to be "only a reader, a peruser" (*TRV,* 6) and because literary images are "sublimations of archetypes" (*TRV,* 4) with a "differential of newness" (*TRV,* 6). Several additional references to complexes and sublimation indicate that Bachelard has not relinquished psychoanalytical allusions, but his interest is not in a reductive treatment of images as symptoms of a hidden subconscious reality, but as the creative continuation of conscious subjective being. Increasingly Bachelard emphasizes the autonomous nature of the literary image as an originator of language. Its purpose, one of "active aestheticism" (*TRV,* 8), is to create being through beauty. Thus the verbal activity of the image is essential to its ontological function.

As Bachelard sees it, the most striking characteristic of earth for the imagination is its resistance to human will. He thus begins by analyzing the images that result from actively working the earth in its various forms, from rock to clay. Here the material and dynamic imaginations are closely related since it is the specific resistance of the material itself that elicits a particular action and its associated reveries. When, in the second part of the book, Bachelard shifts to images of stones, minerals, and gems, he finds that either the dynamic or, especially, the material imagination tends to take precedence separately among such "finished" products of the earth. But, in a concluding section on the psychology of weight, he returns to the theme of falling and rising explored in *L'Air et les songes* and he rediscovers the dynamic imagination associated with earth.

Throughout *La Terre et les rêveries de la volonté* the dynamic imagination is often referred to simply as "will," while the term "imagination" is frequently used to designate the material imagination in particular. In examining the reveries of will when the human hand or tool meets the resistance of the earth, Bachelard writes a panegyric of labor and its psychological benefits: "Work . . . offers a kind of natural psychoanalysis" (*TRV,* 50); "Work is an invertor of hostility" (*TRV,* 59); ". . . as soon as the imagination actualizes its images, the center of being loses its substance of unhappiness" (*TRV,* 20). Work is psychologically healthy because its reveries unite the dynamic and material imaginations in a synthesis of aggression and skill, force and control, that is uniquely human.

Such reveries give dignity to work. "Take away the dreams and you stupefy the worker. . . . Without reveries of will, the will is not really a human force, it is a brutality" (*TRV*, 93). Bachelard even whimsically calls for "a time when each trade will have its certified dreamer, its oneiric guide, where each factory will have its department of poetry!" (*TRV*, 93). Hardly the stuff of Marxism, this. For Bachelard is compelled by images rather than concepts, and such images are born of activity against a resistant matter, not of a detached intellectual perception. When they result from human resistance to earthly gravity, from the dreamed attempt to raise a mountainous mass of earth, these dynamic images translate the "*Atlas complex*" (*TRV*, 372). But, whether dynamic images accompany skilled work against a resistant earth or the more grandiose Atlas Complex, they require the imagined provocation of matter. When the dynamic imagination applies to earth, it is necessarily material.

The Primal Image and Verbal Exuberance

In addition to their synthesis of the dynamic and material imaginations, terrestrial images share with those of other elements a potential for cosmic significance. It matters little if the source of earthly reverie is a humble task, for in the imagination that task can encompass the universe, the red-hot iron of the blacksmith can become the setting sun. In fact, Bachelard finds in this potential for cosmic reverie a means of testing the authenticity of an image. He proposes as a "*hypothesis of reading*" (*TRV*, 157) the question of whether an image can be expected to have cosmic proportions, whether the cosmic and the local can exchange their values. Images with such potential reveal more fundamental "*primal images*" (*TRV*, 158) that have the power to "explain both the universe and man" (*TRV*, 183). In that sense primal images have much in common with myth. They offer an imaginative explanation of how the world came to be, of how the universe exists. They act as "archetypes" (*TRV*, 4), as the source of specific literary images. "In the realm of the literary imagination, a new variation on the oldest of themes is enough to rediscover the action of fundamental dreams" (*TRV*, 275). When a literary image is in touch with its archetypal source in this way, it shares in the universality of myth.

The source of a specific image in a particular writer may well be found in that individual's subconscious, but Bachelard, as was the case with the cultural complexes of *L'Eau et les rêves,* is not interested in such subconscious origins but in their conscious manifestations in literature. An image "can serve dialectically to hide and to display. But one must display much to hide little and it is on the side of this prodigious display that we must study the imagination" (*TRV*, 76). Unlike the psychoanalyst, who concentrates on the action the image has on its producer—on the writer in the case of the literary image—Bachelard proposes to examine "the action it seeks to have on the reader" (*TRV*, 76). This is a significant shift since the focus is less on an individual psyche than on the medium of imagistic activity: on language itself. Through exuberant variations in language, images evoke archetypes or "primal images" and give them continued life. Innovations in the means of expression "tend to free in the reader inert images fixed in the words" (*TRV*, 76). Original images have a beneficial function both for the reader and for language. That they may also benefit the writer is only of incidental interest to Bachelard.

The view of language as a privileged medium whose vitality both depends upon and makes possible imaginative activity is bound to result in some rather definite ideas about the function and practice of literary criticism. Not surprisingly, Bachelard repeatedly protests against the tendency of the established criticism of his day to neglect the full range of imaginative expression and to reduce the literary image to its most obvious rational significance. He insists that *"literary criticism does not have as its function the rationalization of literature.* If it wants to be equal to the literary imagination, it must study *exuberant* expression as well as *restrained* expression"(*TRV*, 320).

His numerous attempts at exegesis in order to classify images begin to modify his original goal of an "objective" approach to the literary image. "A work such as the one we are trying to accomplish, which tries to isolate and classify fundamental material images, cannot, as might be wished, be entirely objective" (*TRV,* 233). Bachelard's experience with the interpretation of images teaches him that, while the goal of objectivity may be maintained, "literary criticism can misjudge" (*TRV,* 320) if rational objectivity is its only aim. The literary critic must be mindful that the literary image may be the source of reverie, that it has a potential for exuberance and expansion which ultimately makes it impossible to classify in absolute terms. "Images do not let themselves be classified like concepts. Even when they are very distinct, they cannot be divided into mutually exclusive types" (*TRV,* 289). At work here is Bachelard's notion of the primacy of the image, including the literary image, and the reverie it provokes. What he discovered a decade earlier in the case of fire continues to apply: even the most rational techniques have their source in the image, and this can include the literary image.

Perhaps it is natural for Bachelard, an intensely private man, to attribute primacy to the image over the concept in literature. The concept, after all, is generated within the context of other concepts and exists by being intellectually accepted by others. It is essentially social. That is much less true for the image, which often originates in isolation, without regard to other images, and which need not be accepted by others in order to exist. "The image, in fact, is less social than the concept, it is more adapted to reveal to us solitary being, the being at the center of its will" (*TRV,* 176). The image is foremost because it expresses the heart of subjective being, before any sort of conceptualization takes place, in short, because it has an ontological function.

The Ontological Function of the Image

If the image contributes to psychological well-being through its dynamism, it is because such activity restores being to its full potential. "The image is always an advancement of being" (*TRV,* 20). This is especially so when the image involves the kind of controlled anger associated with working the earth. With such imagery, "the *human being* is revealed as the *counter being* of things" (*TRV,* 119), which is to say that being increases when the human imagination imposes its will on matter through work. Conversely, we must not lose sight of "the diminution of being brought about by an arrested dynamism" (*TRV,* 374). The fully human reality is an active one for Bachelard, to the point that "passivity is no more than nothingness" (*TRV,* 34). As was the case in *L'Air et les songes,* the dynamic imagination continues to be a determinant of being, especially when it encounters a resistant matter such as earth.

But earth's very materiality also fosters a naive realism of the kind previously associated with the elements of fire and water. This is the case, for example, with metals. Science, even science of first approximation, differentiates between types of metals so that, in fact, this category of matter is a varied one. Yet, for the imagination, which looks at matter naively, such conceptually based diversity is meaningless. "However substantially diverse metals may be, however varied they may be by their weight, their color, their sonority, they still yield a generic material image of metallic existence" (*TRV,* 238). It is this very resistance, this naive reality, this monolithic material hardness, and not the objective and varied reality of science that the dynamic imagination evokes. There exists, therefore, a necessary interplay between the material and dynamic imaginations, although it is quite clear that the essential ontological function is now the province of the dynamic imagination.

An interesting comparison can be drawn here with Bachelard's philosophy of science where naive realism is not only superseded but rejected entirely in the name of an open, constructed science. Whether his concerns are primarily epistemological or ontological, Bachelard clearly is drawn toward openness and dynamism. Indeed, it seems entirely justifiable to suggest that he is attracted by the ontological function of the dynamic imagination precisely *because* his earlier philosophy of science had taught him to appreciate the epistemological function of a dynamic science. Although he shifts his attention from epistemological to ontological considerations, and although he repeatedly recalls the difference between science and poetry, between concept and image, the most fundamental lessons of science, those having to do with the operations of the human psyche, with its openness and profound dynamism, are not forgotten.

In *La Terre et les rêveries de la volonté* the naive realism associated with the material imagination is, therefore, necessarily active. It is inseparable from its counterpart, the active realism of the dynamic imagination. But, like earlier naive realisms, and indeed like active realism itself, it reveals more about the inner being of the imagining subject than about the specific object in question. This is so even though the material imagination often seems to be describing the hidden substance of a particular object. "When someone speaks to you of the *interior* of things, you are sure of hearing disclosures of his own inner secrets" (*TRV, 233*).

This valorization of things by the imagination not only fosters inner being, however. It also enhances the ontological status of the thing itself for the imagining subject, whether he be a writer or a reader. "For the dynamic imagination, there is evidently, beyond the thing, the *superthing,* in the manner in which the ego is dominated by a superego. A piece of wood to which my hand remains indifferent is but a thing, it is even close to being no more than the concept of a thing. But if I whittle it with my knife, that same wood is immediately more than itself, it is a superthing, it assumes all the forces of provocation of a resistant world, it receives naturally all the metaphors of aggression" (*TRV,* 39–40). Here again the parallel with the dynamism and openness of science is rather striking if we recall that the critical objectification resulting from an active, open rationalism led to a determination of a "superobject" (*PN,* 119) typified by the atom. The point is not that there may be similarities between a conceptual superobject and an imagined superthing, but that, undoubtedly influenced by the lessons of science, Bachelard is consistently drawn by a transcendence of immediate static reality. Transposing Sartre, as Bachelard frequently does in *La Terre et les rêveries de la volonté,* we may say that, for Bachelard, dynamic existence precedes superessence.

The comparison with Sartre is instructive in attempting to understand the importance of dynamism in Bachelard's symbolic ontology.[10] Recalling the many images of viscous matter in *Nausea* and Sartre's analysis of viscosity in *Being and Nothingness*, Bachelard points out an important difference between Sartre's "existentialism of real matter and a doctrine of imagined matter" (*TRV*, 115).[11] For Sartre, viscous matter represents an ontological peril, the danger that free human existence can be appropriated by the essential materiality of the world. But Bachelard attributes this perspective to the fact that Sartre does not imagine a dynamic relationship with viscous matter. In Bachelard's estimation Sartre's phenomenology is too visual. "After all, our struggle with viscosity cannot be described by bracketing. Sight alone can 'bracket' " (*TRV*, 116).

Instead, Bachelard proposes a recognition that matter can be worked, that, thanks to the imagination, man need not be passive in the face of a threatening materiality. "Material imagination, in the final analysis, is not dependent upon a phenomenology, but, as we will show on many occasions, on a dynamology" (*TRV*, 117). One of Bachelard's many neologisms, dynamology should not be thought of as the opposite of phenomenology but as an expansion of phenomenology to include the description of the subject's dynamic relationship with the world and the inner transformation such a relationship can bring about. As we saw in Chapter 3, the term is also applied to contemporary science in order to recognize the essential role of energy in any modern metaphysics of matter. Its use as the appropriate ontology in both contexts indicates further that, despite their differences, a fundamental dynamism is common to both scientific and poetic realities for Bachelard.

Where Sartre strives to maintain a separation between subject and object in order to safeguard the inherent freedom of existence, Bachelard actively seeks a confrontation between the two through the dynamic imagination. The result, Bachelard maintains, is not the materialization of free, existing being, feared by Sartre, but the humanization of essential matter. Paradoxically, the active antagonism between subject and object is, for Bachelard, a source of their union. The dynamic imagination transcends the separation between subject and object common to "existentialist" writers. Referring to Albert Camus's *Myth of Sisyphus,* Bachelard insists that when Sisyphus pushes upward with his face against the rock, he does not become a stone, as Camus would have it. Rather, "a rock that receives such a prodigious effort from man is itself already human" (*TRV,* 194). Work humanizes the world so that, in the manner of transcendent science and geometry, a "surexistentialism" transforms the subject-object separation of existentialism:

The imaginary energetics of work strongly unites matter and the worker. The viscous existence of paste is no more than a point of departure, an instigation for a dominated existence. This existence of dominated viscoscity, translated into the energetic imperialism of the subject, is a new example of surexistentialism. This surexistentialism is all the more instructive for dominating an existence of low value by contradicting the first evidence of immediate existence. It posits being in its reaction against both external and internal immediacy. (*TRV,* 121–22)

Surexistentialism, like the superthing, manifests the disposition to transcend immediacy that Bachelard learned from science. As a "philosopher who does not hesitate to take the proofs of his being in his very dreams" (*TRV,* 79), Bachelard attributes ontological status to an inner existence that transcends immediate, concrete reality. It is therefore not surprising that he should be attracted by the surrealists, whose poetry he repeatedly cites. In an observation worthy of André Breton, Bachelard believes that "the imagination does its work far from all functions of supervision, whether that supervision is one of reason, of experience, or of taste" (*TRV,* 320). [12]

But Bachelard also recognizes that not all imaginative activity is so unfettered. Sartre's own more static imagery is a case in point, although it is in the late nineteenth-century writer Joris Karl Huysmans that Bachelard finds the most striking example of a paralyzing imagination that emphasizes immediacy. Sartre's imagery, according to Bachelard, expresses the vertiginous peril of materialization, the subject's *passivity,* the danger of his being engulfed by viscous matter. But Huysmans's imagery reveals a subject who *actively seeks* materialization in a *"petrifying reverie"* (*TRV*, 205) that expresses the subject's willful refusal to participate in the world of living things. Huysmans's images are "illustrations of a *Medusa complex"* (*TRV*, 208), in that they turn all things to stone. Rather than a confrontation of matter through work that unites subject and object by activating subjective being and humanizing the world, the dynamic imagination operates in reverse in Huysmans and actively dehumanizes the world. This results, not in a separation of subject and object, as with the existentialists, but in a reification and paralysis of being that illustrates Bachelard's frequent allusions to the ambivalence of all imagery. Medusa, after all, was also turned to stone by her mirrored gaze.

The ontological consequences of the imagination are quite complex. The dynamic, material imagination may determine subjective inner being, it may designate the inner reality of things, or it may reduce inner being to no more than matter. But in all cases, the reality in question is related to an imagining subject, it is not actual, it is not objectively real. We thus speak of a symbolic ontology. Yet there is another aspect to this question which receives increasing attention from Bachelard, and that is the fact that the images he examines are literary. His focus is on the *"pure literary image"* by which he means "an image that receives all its life from *literature,* or at least an image that remains inert if it does not receive a *prolix* expression" (*TRV*, 321). The verbal exuberance of the literary image is part of its power to evoke. In other words, subjective reality, whether it refers to inner being or outer reality, is both created and expressed by literature. In Bachelard's evolving conception of the literary imagination, the primary ontological function rests with the literary image itself: "the pure literary image is the true *reality of literature.* . . . It would then be interesting to grasp this *literary reality* in its relationship to a well defined *material reality"* (*TRV*, 321). Together with a symbolic ontology dealing with subjective reality through the image, we can now also speak of an ontology of symbol dealing with the specific reality of the literary image and its relationship to material reality.

Earth and Images of Intensity

Like its companion piece on the element of earth, *La Terre et les rêveries du repos* (1948) also espouses the goal of "preparing a doctrine of the literary imagination."[13] Despite the fact that its subtitle announces an *Essay on the Images of Intimacy,* rather than on the imagination of forces, as is the case with the first earth book, the distinctions between imagination and image, or extroverted force and introverted intimacy, are not consistently maintained. To be sure, Bachelard focuses on reveries of intimacy rather than of opposition, but not exclusively so. The preposition *against,* so central to the first earth study, is not forgotten altogether, but, even more significant, is Bachelard's continued preoccupation with the dynamic imagination as a kind of intensity, even when dealing with images of intimacy governed by the preposition *in.* "It is by dreaming about this intimacy that we dream about the repose of being, about an ingrained repose, about a repose that has *intensity* and is not merely that totally external immobility that reigns between inert things" (*TRR,* 5). The title should not mislead us: reveries of repose are anything but static.

In Part One of the book Bachelard explores images of the interior and of depth in the context of the relationship between the material and dynamic imagination. The material imagination's search for inner substance, beyond immediate reality, its unfulfillable yearning to get to the center of things in a final image that would somehow allow the imagination to come to a restful stop is examined in the first chapter. By contrast, the second chapter reintroduces the dynamic imagination, as images of intimacy reveal the role of active struggle. Both imaginations are synthesized in a third chapter where reveries on the qualities of substance disclose that the subject's dynamic will can respond to material images through rhythmical impulses or through the vibrating tension of anticipated action.

The importance attached to literary images of refuge in this study is apparent in the second part where the purely material images of the house, the belly, and the cave are followed by an analysis of the labyrinth as a dynamic image. In a third part this earthly dynamism is further explored with specifically animal and vegetable activations of the labyrinth represented in images of the serpent and the root. A final chapter on "Wine and the Vineyard of the Alchemist" allows Bachelard to conclude his five-volume odyssey of the elemental imagination with a return to the material imagination associated with his native Champagne.

Like its predecessor, this second earth book finds the link between the material and the dynamic imaginations in the very subjectivity of the imagining process. Convinced that "the imagination is nothing other than the subject transported into things" (*TRR, 3*), Bachelard continues to examine this subject-object relationship in terms of its dynamism and necessary materiality. Typical of the material imagination is the attraction toward the inner core of things with which this book is concerned. But specific images such as those of the "labyrinth," which is formed through imagined subterranean motion, and the "serpent," which incorporates earth piercing movement, demonstrate a not uncommon correlation between the material and the dynamic imaginations when images of earth are involved. Moreover, the very desire to pierce the surface of things, to look into the heart of things rather than to be satisfied with the passive, superficial gaze of the formal imagination is itself an aggressive act.

In a brief overview of the imaginative attitudes that command various modes of such dynamic perception, Bachelard identifies four perspectives. In the first, which he calls the "annulled perspective" (*TRV, 9*), depth is an illusion, despite the fact that even science with its goal of objectivity is not bound by such philosophical strictures, that there is "*a chemistry of depths*" (*TRR, 11*) in which substances yield to molecules, molecules to atoms, and atoms to nuclei. The second or "dialectical perspective" (*TRR, 9*) stresses the opposition of the interior and the exterior of things and paradoxically attributes great size to the interior of even the smallest object. Such an imaginative dialectic differs from a rational one in which a "synthesis is offered to conciliate two contrary appearances" (*TRR,* 25–26), since the imagination works analytically as it separates interior depth from surface appearance. The third perspective, which Bachelard calls "an awed perspective" (*TRR,* 9), moves closer to an imagination of inner depth by relating an object's visible qualities, such as color, not only to its substance, as in naive realism, but to its value, as in alchemy. But it is in the fourth perspective of "infinite substantial *intensity*" (*TRR,* 9), that the imagination, following the lead of the alchemist, reaches most profoundly into the interior of objects and, concomitantly, into the heart of the imagining subject. "By dreaming about depth, we dream about our depth. By dreaming about the secret virtue of substances, we dream about our secret being" (*TRR,* 51).

When the imagination chooses to penetrate rather than to work matter, when it seeks the inner depth of things and thus assigns intimate, subjective value to matter, it yearns for an ideal repose, an *"absolute unconsciousness"* (*TRR,* 6). But Bachelard insists that, without consciousness, there can be no material imagination, there can be only matter. Absolute repose is an unattainable ideal for, no matter how intimate the material reverie becomes, there will always be a certain tension between the conscious, imagining subject and the imagined object. Bachelard emphasizes that "the energy of images, their life, does not come . . . from the objects. The imagination is first of all a *toned up subject*" (*TRR,* 87). The French *"sujet tonalisé"* suggests the intensity, the ready dynamism of muscle tone. Even at its most material, when subject and object seem melded, the intensity of the toned-up subject assures that the intimate earth image will be dynamic. The conscious imagination is never content to let an imagined substance simply be.

Naturally, when images of intimacy suggest a struggle beneath the surface of things, the unavoidable dynamism of the imagination is even more obvious. No longer can the material imagination dream of the repose of fixed substance when combat is imagined to be the reality of matter. "The imagination reaches an *ontology of struggle*" (*TRR,* 75) when it acquiesces in such imagery. But, whether images of intimacy lead to a dynamism of tension, as in images of inner repose, or to a dynamism of struggle, as in images of hidden combat, Bachelard is particularly drawn to their ontological perspectives.

In this last book on the elements, Bachelard is especially insistent on the literary expression of such a symbolic ontology. He is not only determined, as before, to study specifically literary images, as opposed to merely psychological ones, he also considers that, in contemporary literature at least, *"the literary image . . . is at the very center of the problem of expression"* (*TRR,* 176). It follows from this view that an examination of the ontological perspective of literary images should yield some insight into the broader ontological status of literature itself. In other words, in *La Terre et les rêveries du repos,* Bachelard edges toward a combination of symbolic ontology, previously associated with the *imagined* reality of the image, and the ontology of symbol, formerly related to the *literary* reality of the image, in order to study the specific reality of literature.

Thus the dynamism which he discovers even in the most material images of repose is largely attributable to the fact that such images are expressed, that "together words and things take on depth" (*TRR,* 12). In discovering the dynamic reality of imagined depth, we also discover the dynamic reality of words themselves. They are inseparable: the reality of imagined depth can exist only through its verbal expression, and the verbal expression can acquire reality, what Sartre calls "substance,"[14] only by referring to imagined depth. In Bachelard's view, when words are considered in this way, they display their capacity to renew language by transcending immediate reality, they reveal a "mythology in action" by tentatively setting forth a new legendary reality: "Through literature, it seems that expression tends toward an autonomy, and even that a conviction is formed, a very light and ephemeral one, to be sure, around a well-made literary image" (*TRR,* 184).[15]

The writer merges image and legend in the literary image in order to compose anew and to particularize an expression of some fundamental archetype that summarizes typical human experiences. Following the lead of C. G. Jung and Robert Desoille, Bachelard asserts that all of us, regardless of our actual lived experiences, carry with us, as part of our imaginative heritage, such archetypal terrestrial images as the house, the refuge, the cave, the labyrinth, the serpent, and the root. As readers we may respond to a literary image conceptually, but it is by awakening the ancient, universal, imaginative responses of the archetype that the literary image is most effectively communicated. Yet for the communication to take place, reading must be sufficiently slowed down, we must "attempt to read texts more slowly still than they were written, as slowly as they were dreamed" (*TRR*, 136). Bachelard assures us that by slowing down our reading in this way, we respond to the "oneiric resonances" (*TRR*, 226) of the image as it strikes an archetypal chord. Such "resonances" must not be stifled, he warns, if the literary image is to be understood.

That such a harmony can exist between the individual literary image and the archetype is another indication that the imagination precedes perception for Bachelard and that it is not only the conceptual narrative reference to concrete reality but the work's subjective reverie that gives value to the image. What makes a harmonic resonance possible between literary image and archetype is their shared subjectivity. Any image can stretch the usual limits of credulity by referring to "*oneiric proofs,*" to "what is *oneirically* possible without being *really* possible" (*TRR*, 130). And such oneiric proofs find their basis in the archetype.

Inspired by Jung, Bachelard proposes that when the archetype is reduced to its most essential characteristics, it reveals a fundamental masculine-feminine duality in which either a masculine *animus* or a feminine *anima* may hold temporary sway by encompassing its opposite. Such is the case, for example, with the "Jonah complex," admittedly a water-related image, but whose reveries of being swallowed and seeking refuge associate it with more distinctly terrestrial imagery. Reduced to schematic proportions, the essence of the complex is revealed as the *animus*-inspired, constructed refuge, represented as a circle within a square, or as the *anima*-inspired and imagined belly, represented as a square within a circle. The archetype reflects the subconscious which "in its most primitive forms, is hermaphroditic" (*TRR*, 149). Bachelard will not develop this idea until he writes *The Poetics of Reverie* some twelve years later, but it is worth noting, in passing, that both the constructive *animus* and the dreaming *anima* have their counterpart in literary images with their "double perspective of dreams and thoughts" (*TRR*, 130).

The literary image, then, is both a dreamed image and a conceptual, narrated image. And it is consistent with Bachelard's notion of a Copernican revolution of the imagination, in which subjective imagination precedes objective perception, that reverie should be experienced subjectively before being narrated. The labyrinth, for example, is not foreseen as a totality in reverie, but is created as the dreaming subject moves through the dream. It is only after the fact, when the dream is related, that the labyrinth can be "seen." In an apt metaphor, Bachelard suggests that "Ariadne's thread is the thread of oration. It belongs to the order of narrated dream. It is a thread that retraces" (*TRR*, 215).[16] There are, therefore, two "moments" to the creation of a literary image which correspond, first to reverie, then to narration.

This emphasis on the process by which the literary image is communicated marks the beginning of a new direction in Bachelard's thinking. It is made possible by the gradual discovery, throughout the *Elements,* that the image is not just an indicator of subjective being but that it has a related ontological status as expression. The question, which Bachelard only begins to address in *La Terre et les rêveries du repos,* and which will preoccupy him in his subsequent books on the imagination, then becomes one of how the specific reality of the image can be *known,* given its combined subjective and objective being.

Chapter Seven

A Phenomenology of the Creative Imagination

During most of the decade following *La Terre et les rêveries du repos,* Bachelard returned to his original concerns with the publication of his epistemological trilogy—*Le Rationalisme appliqué, L'Activité rationaliste de la physique contemporaine,* and *Le Matérialisme rationnel*—on the dialectic of rationalism and empiricism. But what may be termed Bachelard's "ontological vacation," during which he wrote the *Elements,* was not without its influence on the epistemological questions he confronted in this subsequent period. As we saw earlier, when he came back to the philosophy of science, Bachelard faced the question of whether science could lead to an ontology. The qualified answer that science leads to "ontogenesis" and "dynamology" is one that respects the actuality of science but that does not seem to satisfy Bachelard's metaphysical longings quite as completely as does the poetic imagination. Not surprisingly, he eventually returns to the symbolic ontology of the imagination, only this time, he is determined to treat the imagination on its own terms, to give it the philosophy it merits. Having drawn a philosophy of science from the actual activity of science, Bachelard may be said to repeat the process with respect to the imagination.

A Nonreductive Philosophy of Reading

When we consider Bachelard's difficulty in coming to a systematic doctrine of the imagination in the *Elements,* we are better able to understand why his choice of a phenomenological approach to the literary imagination is a most appropriate one. For phenomenology, with its array of meanings, must be applied to be understood; it is a method, an approach, at least as much as it is a doctrine. In setting out to develop a "phenomenology of the imagination" (*PS*, xiv) in the *Poetics of Space,* Bachelard places his thought in a particular philosophical context without forcing the literary image into the strait jacket of a priori theory. Like other phenomenologists, beginning with Husserl, he proposes to apprehend the phenomenon (in this case, the literary image) non-empirically and without reference to its causes. His reasons for doing so are grounded in his previous ontological discoveries, which revealed the essential autonomy of the literary image. Bachelard is now more willing to consider the possibility that a "philosophy of poetry" (*PS*, xi), unlike science, would not be based on logical relations and axiomatic principles but would actually be renewed by each image. In *The Poetics of Space* he defines the means of such a renewal, namely the phenomenology of the imagination, as "a study of the phenomenon of the poetic image when it emerges into the consciousness as a direct product of the heart, soul and being of man, apprehended in its actuality" (*PS*, xiv), and as a "consideration of the *onset of the image* in an individual consciousness" (*PS*, xv).

But the phenomenological approach is not only contrasted to the epistemology of science but to the "scientific prudence" (*PS*, xiv) of the *Elements,* where Bachelard claims to have remained faithful to the requirements of the philosophy of science by avoiding any personal interpretation of the image. Yet it has already been pointed out that he rejects conceptual, positivistic methods of analysis throughout the *Elements* as well, and that, as early as the *Psychoanalysis of Fire,* he is concerned with avoiding overly rational approaches that would threaten the unconscious source of the literary imagination. It might thus be more accurate to speak merely of the taxonomic rather than the scientific prudence of the *Elements* since Bachelard's classification of images according to the four elements as well as his distinctions between the formal, material, and the dynamic imaginations allow him to speculate on the conditions for the existence of the poetic image without being excessively concerned with how a reader may apprehend that image. His phenomenology is not altogether new, but whatever difference it does have with the *Elements* stems from the fact that it rejects one of two "objectivities": the framework of objectivity grounded in psychology and psychoanalysis, or of the illusion of objectivity stemming from his taxonomy of the imagination. Both objectivity and its illusion ultimately prove to be unsatisfactory approaches to the literary image.

In the manner of phenomenologists, Bachelard now may be said to "bracket" or exclude objective references to concrete reality along with any attempt to ascertain the role of the image within the overall composition of the work. It is not that such tasks are unnecessary in Bachelard's view, only that they are secondary to the initial apprehension of the image. To proceed directly to such ancillary questions would destroy through reduction what, for Bachelard, is the fundamental reality of literature: the literary image itself. As he sees it, phenomenology is opposed to the empirical reduction of an image to something outside itself [1] because of its method, "which consists of designating the image as an excess of the imagination" (*PS,* 112). Such a method recognizes an essential exaggeration in the image and proposes that the reader may best apprehend that image by exaggerating it further. "The phenomenological gain appears right away: in prolonging *exaggeration,* we may have the good fortune to avoid the habits of *reduction*" (*PS,* 219). The exaggeration in Bachelard's phenomenological method operates in opposition to the reductive techniques of psychoanalysis, whose role has been diminished.

As he had begun to do increasingly within the taxonomic framework of the *Elements*, Bachelard now concentrates more freely on specific types of images. The link between these images is the use of space as refuge, and, if there is one overriding image, it is certainly that of the house. Bachelard had previously examined the "native house" of memory and the archetypal "oneiric house" in *La Terre et les rêveries du repos* (95–128). He now adds the unattainable "dream house" (*PS,* 61) to this principal image of refuge as it guides his examination of the still more intimate imaginative space of drawers, trunks, nests, and seashells. After three chapters on the dialectical spatial relationships represented in the opposition of large and small, inside and outside, or open and closed, Bachelard concludes with a chapter on "The Phenomenology of Roundness" which epitomizes the self-sufficient, non-referent character of his phenomenology.

Since the purpose of his phenomenology is to approach the *literary* image (now increasingly referred to as the *poetic* image), there is a renewed and increased emphasis on the central function of reading—including the slow, deliberate reading suggested in *La Terre et les rêveries du repos*—as a means of allowing the reader's imagination to develop the potentialities of the image. Even more representative of Bachelard's phenomenology is his insistence on a second or third reading "that will give us the illusion of participating in the work of the author of the book" (*PS*, 21). This emphasis on reading, on the apprehension of the image as a means of reliving the creative process itself, indicates how Bachelard's phenomenology complements the *Elements* while remaining distinct in approach. The second or third reading is the Ariadne's thread of the phenomenologist. It parallels precisely Bachelard's description of narration, in *La Terre et les rêveries du repos*, as the thread permitting a return through the labyrinth of the writer's initial imaginative experience.

From Topoanalysis to Reverberation

Because Bachelard's phenomenology is best understood in its application to specific literary images, it is possible to abstract certain principles form his practice as well as from his commentary. Foremost among these is the notion that imagination gives value to space and that such qualified spaces can be studied. With his usual predisposition to coinage, Bachelard calls this study "topoanalysis," which, he suggests, could be an "auxiliary of psychoanalysis" (*PS*, 8), but which, in practice, becomes a phenomenological analysis of space, a means of inquiring into intimate space, into how space is imagined. It is, as he points out, a "hermeneutics" (*PS*, 9) since it is unconcerned with the causal questions of biography, but concentrates instead on the interpretive analysis of literary space imagery.

While he recognizes the possibility of hostile spatial imagery, Bachelard chooses to examine only those images in which man is at one with the world, a predilection for happy space which he labels "topophilia" (*PS,* xxxi). Both coinages, topoanalysis and topophilia, taken together refer to Bachelard's attempt to "bracket" references to geometric spacial reality, as such, by insisting on an examination of valorized space expressed in images of spatial well-being. Bachelard's topophilia is a recognition that, unlike the quantifiable, neutral space of geometry, a lived-in space acquires qualities for the imagination. Rational spatial measurements do not apply to imagined space where size may be inverted and the minuscule may loom large, and where geometrically neutral oppositions between interior and exterior may lose their symmetrical reciprocity as one is preferred over the other. When reverie replaces reason as an integrating principle, Bachelard observes, a corner has the makings of a house and a house can become a universe.

Such images seem naive when seen from a rational or commonsense perspective, but it is just such "naive wonder" (*PS,* 93) that the phenomenological approach seeks to awaken in the reader. The image cannot be apprehended conceptually because it would vanish in the attempt. It can be grasped only through a shared wonderment between poet and reader which recognizes the image's "quality of inter-subjectivity" (*PS,* xx). Just as concepts are means of rational communication, so the images can be means by which reveries are communicated. In *La Terre et les rêveries du repos,* Bachelard had suggested that images were transmitted by awakening certain "resonances" within underlying archetypes. When he returns to the idea of resonances in *The Poetics of Space,* it is to emphasize the exuberance and multiplicity of reactions to the poetic image. This is perfectly in keeping with his phenomenological approach as is the related, though distinct, notion of "reverberation," which he borrows from Eugène Minkowski.[2]

As conceived in *The Poetics of Space,* resonance refers to the image's awakening of sentimental, surface exuberance, which in turn stirs archetypal echoes. It describes the reaction of *Geist* or "mind" to the image. Reverberation, on the other hand, describes the image's capacity to elicit responses directly from the depth of being, from the *Seele* or "soul." Here Bachelard borrows terms from German philosophy where, he claims, "the distinction between mind and soul (*der Geist und die Seele*) is so clear" (*PS*, xvi). Either resonance or reverberation represents a possible direction of phenomenological analysis, although, in still another limitation of his approach, Bachelard chooses to concentrate primarily on the phenomenon of reverberation. The choice is not arbitrary since, of the two, reverberation is the only one that can provide access to the "poetic power rising naively within us" (*PS*, xix). It is the only one through which the reader marvels at the *individual* poetic image, the only one through which the image is communicated *directly* from subject to subject. Through reverberation one can "find the real measure of the being of a poetic image" (*PS*, xii) because nothing else interferes with the image's specific reality.

In applying his phenomenological principles, Bachelard allows certain literary images to reverberate within his own reader's soul, with minimal reference to extraneous conceptual systems such as psychology and psychoanalysis. The purpose of this process is to allow him to make, or to confirm, observations about the essential nature of the literary image. Yet there remains within Bachelard a predisposition to consider even a purposefully naive phenomenological reading within a larger philosophical context. His goal remains a "metaphysics of the imagination" (*PS*, xiv), and his focus is on the *"direct ontology"* (*PS*, xii) of the image as it is apprehended by the reader: "the reader of poems is asked to consider an image not as an object and even less as the substitute for an object, but to seize its *specific reality*" (*PS*, xv, emphasis added). This evident metaphysical orientation undergirds Bachelard's phenomenology in both *The Poetics of Space* and the subsequent *Poetics of Reverie* so that ontological questions are primary while his phenomenology develops as the only means to apprehend the image without destroying its specific reality.

But if it is neither an object nor an object substitute, what is the reality of the image that Bachelard's phenomenology reveals?

Some of the features of the image had been identified in the *Elements* and, as before, the image is seen as primary, as preceding not only perception but thought itself. It is just such a direct connection with the prereflective soul of being that makes phenomenology an especially appropriate approach to the image in Bachelard's estimation. Related to its primacy is the image's simplicity, which also has much to do with Bachelard's preference for a willfully naive phenomenology over more systematic conceptual approaches. "The image, in its simplicity, has no need for scholarship" (*PS*, xv), he maintains, so that "a phenomenologist should go in the direction of maximum simplicity" (*PS*, 107).

Bachelard also insists with fresh vigor on the radical newness of the image. Severed from any cause, it is viewed as an essentially unexpected phenomenon of language, an emergence of language, which, because it cannot be detemined, "is essentially *variational*, and not, as in the case of the concept, *constitutive*" (*PS*, xv). This element of surprise would, of course, be lost if the image were subjected to the conceptual scrutiny of traditional literary criticism *before* it could be apprehended in its specific reality. What Bachelard's phenomenology attempts to preserve is the uncaused, unexpected character of an image with no necessary links to a psychological past. Thus he refers to images as being "metapsychological" (*PS*, 233), or beyond the psychological, in the way metaphysics transcends the physical. In a comment on Bachelard's use of this term, apparently borrowed from Freud, Gabriel Germain draws an enlightening parallel between the radical newness of the image, cut off from the past, and the view of time as disconnected instants which Bachelard had proposed in *L'Intuition de l'instant*.[3] Such a correspondence draws attention to the fact that, while a quarter of a century separates the two texts, Bachelard's ontology consistently tends toward the atomistic.

We have seen that *L'Intuition de l'instant*, written when Bachelard was still primarily interested in the epistemology of science, evinced a longing for ontology. Is there a complementary nostalgia for epistemology even when Bachelard's avowed purpose is to discard the methods of science in dealing with the image and when his text is full of the vocabulary of metaphysics? What would be the significance of any such nostalgia? Before an answer to these questions can be attempted, it is necessary to examine Bachelard's last major work of phenomenology: *The Poetics of Reverie.*

A Phenomenology of Poetic Reverie

Toward the end of *The Poetics of Reverie* (1960) Bachelard asks:

> If a Poetics of Reverie could be constructed, it would uncover examination procedures which would allow us to study the activity of the imagination systematically. . . . Through poetry, reverie becomes positive, becomes an activity which ought to interest the psychologist.
>
> Without following the poet into his deliberately *poetic* reverie, how will one make up a psychology of the imagination? Will he take documents from those who do not imagine, who forbid themselves to imagine, who "reduce" the abundant images to a stable idea, from those—more subtle negators of the imagination—who "interpret" images, ruining all possibility of an ontology of images and a phenomenology of the imagination at the same time?[4]

If Bachelard continues to find it desirable to maintain an ontology of the image and a phenomenology of the imagination, it is because, taken together, both allow the image to be apprehended as a specific imaginative reality without recourse to the image-destructive measures of reductive analysis, be they those of psychoanalysis or conceptual literary criticism.

The Poetics of Reverie represents Bachelard's attempt to give procedural coherence to his phenomenology without falling back into the trap of reductionism. The key to this attempt, the guiding principle of the phenomenology of this second *Poetics* is the coherence of poetry itself. When the image is a *poetic* image, it is not merely part of a free-floating reverie; it is given positive value because of its controlled use within the language of the poem. For this reason, it is not simply reverie but *poetic* reverie that interests Bachelard in this essay. As he explains in his introduction: "In speaking of a *Poetics of Reverie,* when the simple title 'Poetic Reverie' had been tempting me for a long time, I

wanted to indicate the force of coherence which a dreamer feels
when he is really faithful to his dreams, and that his dreams take
on coherence precisely because of their poetic qualities" (*PR,*
15–16). Where the *Poetics of Space* develops phenomenological
principles through their application to specific types of images,
the *Poetics of Reverie* is more of an abstract, though by no means
philosophically doctrinaire discourse on the phenomenology of
poetic reverie or, as Bachelard puts it, "a poetics of poetic reverie"
(*PR,* 16).

Having established his distance from the reductive methods
of psychoanalysis and psychology in *The Poetics of Space*, Bachelard
now allows himself to consider anew—but from a phenomenological perspective, that is, from a perspective that respects the
reality of the image—questions of the psychology of the imagination. He unhesitatingly makes use of the lessons of depth
psychology, particularly that of Jung, not to reduce images to
a hidden reality, but to examine the *"absolute sublimation"* (*PR,*
58) or idealized transformation of that reality into the words of
the poem. This procedure leads him, once again, to the androgy-
nous basis of the human psyche, particularly to its idealizing
principle: the reverie associated with *anima.*

Animus and Anima

The reader familiar with Bachelard's earlier work will know
that the Jungian distinction between *animus* and *anima,* first
proposed in *La Terre et les rêveries du repos,* refers to the deep-seated
duality in the psyche of men and women alike. This duality is
at the source of the human disposition to organize and make
projects (*animus*), and the equally human inclination to imagine
and daydream (*anima*). Upon returning to this notion in *The
Poetics of Reverie,* Bachelard stresses in particular the value of the
anima, which has its own powers despite the apparent relative
strength of the *animus.* Either principle can reveal psychological
verities, but the *anima,* in stressing the potential for openness
and receptivity in human nature, is especially suited to a phenomenological approach and, more particularly, to an exploration
of poetic reverie.

For reverie, or daydream, like the *anima* principle, reflects the feminine side of the human psyche in both men and women. As such it is opposed to nocturnal dream, which is solitary and unconscious. Despite the arbitrary origin of grammatical gender, Bachelard is obviously encouraged in this view by the fact that "dream" (*le rêve* or *le songe*) is masculine in French, while "daydream" (*la rêverie*) is feminine. Yet he claims that the feminine sense of reverie is ascertainable "beyond the words" (*PR*, 18), that is, beyond the mere fact of grammatical gender. As he sees it, reverie is not a derivative of dream but a necessary and distinct element of a well-balanced human psyche. That difference stems from two main attributes of reverie: (1) it is communicated and relived through writing and (2) it allows consciousness to intervene. The dream, on the other hand, makes for dull recitation with none of the poetry of written reverie.

But, in pursuing his goal of examining reverie rather than dream, Bachelard insists on an approach that will not lose sight of both the masculine and feminine aspects of the human psyche. It is a question of studying "a reverie which places a dreamed communion of *animus* and *anima,* the two principles of the integral being, in the soul of a dreamer of human values" (*PR*, 91). Only a reverie on reverie, a nonconceptual, phenomenological approach seems suitable, for Bachelard is convinced that "the concept would stifle [the] life" (*PR*, 52) of the poetic images that bring about reverie. "The image can only be studied through the image, by dreaming images as they gather in reverie. It is a non-sense to claim to study imagination objectively since one really receives the image only if he admires it" (*PR*, 53). The resulting separation of image and concept, on which Bachelard insists, is a continuation of the opposition of reverie and dream, *anima* and *animus,* and ultimately, of poetry and science, which, as we now see, is necessary from the perspectives of both activities. Bachelard makes clear that the fundamental error of the alchemist was just such a "false union of the concept and the image" (*PR*, 77). The image cannot lead to the concept without distorting thought, and the image cannot be examined by the concept without being distorted.[5]

The purpose of Bachelard's approach to the poetic image is to maintain in the reader the poet's reverie which the image both expresses and fosters. "Poetic images stimulate our reverie; they melt into our reverie because the power of assimilation of the *anima* is so great. . . . An image received in the *anima* puts us in a state of continuous reverie" (*PR*, 65). Critical reading, what Bachelard calls "reading in *animus*," is not up to such a task. Only "reading in *anima*" has the receptivity required, not just to maintain, but to continue the poetic image in the reverie of the reader. Reading in *anima* is, clearly, phenomenological reading.

The Metaphysics of Reverie

Bachelard identifies three attributes of reverie that make such phenomenological reading possible. The first involves an almost Proustian remembrance of the "nucleus of childhood" (*PR*, 100) which poetry can revive. Such a return to childhood clearly has nothing to do with psychoanalytical recollection. Instead, facts or events recalled by the *animus*-inspired memory are given value by the *anima*-inspired imagination. "In order to relive the *values of the past*, one must dream, must accept the great dilation of the psyche known as reverie" (*PR*, 105). Such a past, like the poetic image itself, is admired rather than perceived. Its recreation through reverie renews a childhood sense of wonder that is essential to any reading in *anima*.

The second attribute of reverie examined by Bachelard, the fact that it can be conscious of itself, is essential to the value of reverie as a phenomenological tool when associated with reading, since subjective consciousness is a sine qua non of phenomenological activity. As we have indicated, it is this possibility of consciousness that distinguishes reverie from nocturnal dream:

And here is the radical difference for us between the nocturnal dream (*rêve*) and reverie, the radical difference, a difference deriving from phenomenology; while the dreamer of the nocturnal dream is a shadow who has lost his self (*moi*), the dreamer of reverie, if he is a bit philosophical, can formulate a *cogito* at the center of his dreaming self (*son moi rêveur*). Put another way, reverie is an oneiric activity in which a glimmer of consciousness subsists. The dreamer of reverie is present in his reverie. *(PR, 150)*

Bachelard, of course, is certainly "a bit philosophical," even as a dreamer and, as he had done before, he borrows the Cartesian ontological formula, *cogito ergo sum*, to examine the metaphysical consequences of a phenomenological reverie. The *cogito* implies a subject who is aware of his thinking activity, from which stems, in turn, an awareness of his existence as a separate subject. When Bachelard attempts to apply the *cogito* to dream, he discovers an unaware, undifferentiated subject in the case of nocturnal dream, but a self-aware subject in the case of reverie.

Bachelard considers reverie to be "poetic," in the etymological sense of "creative," because it adds to the subject's being by fixing on a specific image that mediates between the subject and the world. As he indicates: "Reverie assembles being around its dreamer" with the result that "the philosophical study of reverie calls us to nuances of ontology" *(PR, 152)*. Unlike the "strong ontology" *(PR, 166)* of traditional philosophy, he proposes a "differential ontology" *(PR, 167)* that would take into account the interpenetration of subject and object that takes place in reverie. For the daydreamer, be he poet or reader, is conscious both of his own subjective being and of a subjectively viewed world, to the point that one is an enhancement and confirmation of the other. Applied to reverie, Descartes's *cogito* is transformed into a new formula: "I dream the world, therefore, the world exists as I dream it" *(PR, 158)*. In reverie there need be no opposition between the subject and the world. Where objectivity requires the subject to accommodate itself to a rationally organized physical reality, resulting in a separation of subject and object, self-aware reverie accommodates the world to subjective reality, thus transcending the subject-object opposition without destroying the separate identity of the subject. At work here, as Bachelard frequently reminds his reader, is the "irreality function."

Quoting an observation of Henri Bosco, one of his favorite poetic sources in *The Poetics of Reverie,* Bachelard indicates that "all the being of the world, if it dreams, dreams that it is speaking" (*PR,* 187). The link between the dreamer and the world is language, and the world thus conceived is spoken and anthropomorphic. Bachelard sees this linguistic subjectivity as a fundamental and original feature of reverie, one that predates our scientific culture. In giving voice to the world, reverie takes on a cosmic quality which he identifies as its third major attribute.[6] Such language creates a "cosmic image" (*PR,* 175) that makes of the world and of the dreaming subject a stable, unified, universal being. Returning to the inspiration of the *Elements,* Bachelard maintains that this is especially so "when the reverie unifies cosmos and substance" (*PR,* 176), something that is particularly likely to happen when an archetypal primal image is at work. Yet such references to earlier works merely support the essential point that "there are cosmic words, words which give man's being to the being of things" (*PR,* 189).

Inevitably, it seems, Bachelard's consideration of reverie leads him, despite his occasional disavowals of philosophical intentions, to a preoccupation with ontological considerations, whether these are identified as the "penumbral ontology" (*PR,* 111) of childhood, the "differential ontology" of the dreamer's *cogito,* or the "ontology of the imagination" (*PR,* 200) associated with cosmic reverie. The common thread linking these ontologies is their philosophical idealism. All three are associated with the various attributes of reverie which Bachelard specifically identifies with idealism when he states as a goal of *The Poetics of Reverie,* "the precise task of studying the idealizing reverie" (*PR,* 91). In fact, one reason Bachelard takes his examples from literature rather than from life is that the poet transforms reality into an idealized image which then has the power to idealize objective reality for the reader. "The poet gives the real object its imaginary double, its idealized double. This idealized double is immediately idealizing, and it is thus that a universe is born from an expanding image" (*PR,* 176).

Reverie, which culminates in the poetic word, is both idealizing and free. It is not determined by immediate commonsense experience; rather, it creates the world along with the subject. In this sense, we can speak of a subjective idealism in Bachelard since subjectivity is essential to the idealist or symbolic ontology of the image, essential to what Bachelard calls "the realization of an effective idealization in *animus* and *anima* (*PR*, 92). It is perfectly consistent with this idealist stance for Bachelard to discard biographical and psychoanalytical approaches to literature. When he proclaims that "I shall never be anything but a psychologist of books" (*PR*, 93), he is not stating his adherence to psychological realism, to the psychology of the author, but to the psychology of the work, to the idealist consideration of "poetic works as effective human realities" (*PR*, 92). Science has taught us that what had once passed as reality was in fact an illusion. Bachelard makes a virtue of this adversity by approaching the illusion phenomenologically, as the "realization of an idealization." Metaphysically, such an idealized reality still calls for an ontology, as *The Poetics of Reverie* makes clear. But it may be asked if it also calls for an epistemology.

An Ineluctable Epistemology

The notion that either of the *Poetics,* where the emphasis on ontology is so obvious, is also a work of epistemology may seem outlandish at first. This is especially so if Bachelard's several claims that he is rejecting knowledge, or learning (*savoir*), in favor of phenomenology prevent the reader from considering both the purpose of such a phenomenology and the subversive influence of an epistemological outlook of long standing. Our analysis of *The Poetics of Space* has already raised the question of an epistemological longing in the late works on the imagination. A closer examination of the text of both *Poetics* reveals a clear influence of the epistemological outlook at the very moment Bachelard seeks to reject its guidance.

What is being suggested here is not a denial of the essential difference between science and poetry; indeed Bachelard's consistency in insisting on the difference between the two demonstrates his fundamental understanding of the special nature of each endeavor. But such an understanding does not preclude a philosophical approach, including an application of questions of epistemology and ontology, to both science and poetry. We have already seen how Bachelard confronted the ontological questions posed by science in his essays on applied rationalism which followed the *Elements*. What we are now suggesting is that Bachelard, despite his overt attention to ontology in both *Poetics,* and without losing sight of the difference between science and poetry, is guided by a philosophical perspective which, in part at least, grows out of his epistemology of science.

In introducing the notion of the dreamer's *cogito* in *The Poetics of Reverie,* Bachelard apologizes for his use of philosophical jargon by explaining that "it is difficult for a philosopher to tear himself away from his long-time habits of thought" (*PR,* 21). The echo of his philosophy is deliberate here, but the explanation could apply to countless other, apparently inadvertent references, throughout his *Poetics,* not only to jargon but to points of view stemming from his earlier epistemology. Surely reverie's idealization beyond common-sense experience recalls the transcendence of a science of second approximation. The idealism of reverie is subjective, to be sure, yet would a narrowly positivistic philosopher of science, unschooled in the lessons of contemporary physics, be as receptive as Bachelard to the possibility of a "differential ontology"? Bachelard's "conversion to the imaginary" may not have taken place quite so readily if he had not recognized the requirement that philosophy tread lightly on the object of its inquiry, a lesson he learned from science.

It is this respect for the specific reality of his analysis that enables Bachelard to recognize a "Copernican revolution of the imagination" which parallels the Copernican revolution of abstraction." Yet it should not be surprising that a rationalist like Bachelard should realize that the poetic image is uncaused, for he was never a dogmatic rationalist to begin with. We have seen that he took his lessons from the interplay of the rational and the empirical in contemporary science. He was disposed by his work in the epistemology of science to be wary of a priori, universal, and fixed logical categories, a disposition that allowed him to respond to the inventive images of surrealism so well.

The point becomes clearer when we consider several specific instances in which Bachelard applies a perspective learned from his philosophy of science to his metaphysics of the imagination. In *L'Expérience de l'espace en physique contemporaine* and again in *La Formation de l'esprit scientifique,* Bachelard had emphasized the contemporary scientific principle which holds that position and motion cannot be simultaneously determined. Rather than the stable, localized geometric space of Cartesian philosophy and Newtonian physics, the experiments of contemporary science lead to a nondeterministic notion of space. But just as the "experiment of space" in contemporary physics was shown to transcend the commonsense, geometric "experience of space," the imagination of space requires a similar transcendence in poetry. As Bachelard points out in *The Poetics of Space,* "the dialectics of outside and inside is supported by a reinforced geometrism, in which limits are barriers. We must be free as regards all *definitive* intuitions— and geometrism records definitive intuitions—if we are to follow the daring of the poets (as we shall do later) who invite us to the finesses of experiences of intimacy, to 'escapades' of imagination" (*PS*, 215). Like Pascal, whose dual interest in science and poetry Bachelard inevitably evokes, he identifies, without using the precise terms, an *esprit de géometrie* and an *esprit de finesse,* although with Bachelard, it is science that initially teaches the need for such an *esprit de finesse.*[7]

Science had also taught him the necessity of incorporating possibility into any rational construction of reality. We have seen in a previous chapter that, as early as *Le Nouvel Esprit scientifique,* he had pondered the parallel between the mathematics of possibilities and poetry.[8] Similarly, in *The Poetics of Reverie,* Bachelard stresses the possibilities for the renewal of subjective being inherent in the language of poetry. The imagination does not reflect the present or the past but opens the way to the multiple possibilities of the future through poetic reverie. "A world takes form in our reverie, and this world is ours. This dreamed world teaches us the possibilities for expanding our being within our universe. There is a *futurism* in any dreamed universe" (*PR*, 8). It is precisely such possibilities, in both science and poetry, that a flexible finesse, as opposed to a rigid geometry, can recognize.

Bachelard considers himself to be engaged not only in a metaphysics of imagined being, whose concrete counterpart would be a physics of objective reality, but, as he puts it in *The Poetics of Reverie,* in "a micrometaphysical study of the being which appears and disappears only to reappear, following the undulations of a reverie on being" (*PR,* 111). The objective counterpart that is suggested here is clearly contemporary microphysics, despite the fact that Bachelard never confuses the specific reality of imagined and objective being. Far from being based on an illusory notion of a shared reality between science and poetry, the parallel is grounded in the implicit recognition that the philosophical lessons of science, which can be summarized as the need for an open, flexible philosophy, adaptable to the continuous revolutions of science, are equally applicable to the aesthetic revolution of contemporary literature. Both science and literature require not only their own ontology, whether it is called "dynamology" or "differential ontology," but their own epistemology as well.

Bachelard's phenomenology is his epistemological response to literature; it is the means of *knowing* the literary image, adapted to the specific circumstances of that image's existence, in the way his epistemology of science was adapted to the unique features of contemporary scientific reality. Such a phenomenology is as capable of revealing obstacles to the imagination as his epistemology of science had been able to point out obstacles to knowledge, or "epistemological obstacles." In *The Poetics of Space,* for example, Bachelard calls attention to the excessive clarity of some images, whose counterpart in science would be the excessive generalization of certain concepts: "Images that are too clear . . . become generalities, and for that reason block the imagination" (*PS,* 121). Bachelard's phenomenology of the imagination is as sensitive to the delicate relationship between how we know and what we know as had been his epistemology of science. A constant factor, and a unifying force of his work, is the necessary interplay of epistemology and ontology. This "mere reader" never really ceases to be a philosopher.

Candlelight and Solitary Reverie

It is somehow fitting that *La Flamme d'une chandelle* (1961), a reverie on flame and light, should be the last published work of a man who began his career with an epistemological study of the science of thermodynamics and who embarked upon his exploration of the imagination under the sign of fire. Yet, from the very first line, Bachelard announces his intention of writing a "little book of simple reverie, without the surcharge of any knowledge, without imprisoning myself in the unity of a method of inquiry."[9] Gone are references to psychoanalysis and even to psychology and, while the "consciousness of reverie" (*FC*, 10) associated with this in-*anima* meditation on candleflame preserves all the features of the phenomenology developed in the *Poetics*, phenomenology itself is not overtly evoked.

Yet it would be a mistake to see in this delightful book of reverie, this *"Poetry of Flames"* (*FC*, 4) as Bachelard also calls it, a change in direction from the *Poetics*. In the first place, it was initially conceived as a segment of a larger work, to have been entitled, significantly enough, *"The Poetics of Fire"* (*FC*, 5). This third volume of the *Poetics* was never published, although the existence of a manuscript entitled *La Poétique du Phénix* has since been revealed.[10] Second, Bachelard's rejection of rationalistic knowledge in seeking to apprehend the image is itself a continuation of the outlook of the *Poetics*, where the frame of reference was broadly philosophical. *La Flamme d'une chandelle* is a book in which, as Bachelard himself points out, "it is not science, but philosophy that dreams" (*FC*, 14). His reference to a "physics of value" which replaces a "physics of facts" (*FC*, 61) when dealing with the poetry of Novalis is a reminder that the unspoken phenomenological approach of *La Flamme d'une chandelle* continues to be allied with a metaphysics of the imagination. As in the *Poetics*, he continues to think of himself as a "simple philosopher of the literary expression" (*FC*, 26).

The emphasis throughout is on the solitude required of the dreamer of the literary image, whether writer or reader. Alone at a candlelit table with a book or a blank page, or merely lost in the reverie of the candle's solitary flame as the result of some poetic image, the dreamer derives a "security of being" (*FC*, 7) from the candle's flame as it imagistically reveals the play of darkness and light within the conscious reverie. The flame, both solitary and vertical, seemingly attracted upwards by light, leads the dreamer, in a phenomenological reverie on reverie, to reflect on his own solitary reverie, which is attracted by the poetic image. Such phenomenological observations contribute to "an ontology of solitary being" (*FC*, 13) on the one hand, and justify themselves as approaches to the image, on the other. As he had frequently done before, Bachelard points out that a less naive, more conceptual critical approach to the image is not able to respect the singularity of each image, is not able to respond to the image's call to reverie and to its lively immediacy. To develop a critical explanation of an image "would be to slow down, to stop the impetus of [the] imagination" (*FC*, 72). Images are inextricably linked to the words that express them; they are "sentence images" or "poetic maxims" that require immediate adhesion rather than conceptual analysis.

Yet in an epilogue recounting his own solitude, seated at his work table between the familiar lamp and the hostile white page, Bachelard admits to a nostalgia for conceptual thinking after his long vacation of reverie. The *Poetics,* including the fragment entitled *La Flamme d'une chandelle,* have set right the overly rational taxonomy of the *Elements* by working out a means of apprehending the image that promotes rather than reduces its being. The epistemological problem raised by the image's symbolic ontology has found a resolution in Bachelard's phenomenology. His hope now is to complete the tableau by turning his philosophical interests once again to the rigors of science. But the flickering candle, lighting the solitary evening of his years, is forever to remain his characteristically humble farewell.

Chapter Eight
Conclusion

The philosophical implications of how contemporary science comes to know phenomena preoccupy Bachelard from the outset and continue to engross him well after he begins his work on the literary imagination. His epistemological interests are so profound that they inevitably provide the context for his philosophy of the imagination. Of course, Bachelard recognizes essential methodological differences between the two activities as well as the disparate realities—science and poetry—with which each must deal. But, despite his conscious and wholly justified effort to keep science and poetry apart in order to be faithful to each, there is in Bachelard a subtle "cross-fertilization" from the philosophy of one domain to that of the other. This is not a failure. Rather, it demonstrates the suppleness of Bachelard's intelligence in transferring the most essential lessons of one realm to the other without denying the distinctiveness of each.

Such transference is made possible by a philosophical approach, with its articulation of epistemology and ontology, that consciously seeks to respect the particularities of the object of scrutiny by avoiding a priori characterization. This constant feature of Bachelard's philosophical method allows him to discover certain complementarities between science and poetry, including a similar dynamism and openness. It also leads to an assessment of the role of imagination in science as a means of linking reason and reality and of incorporating future-oriented possibilities within the rational system. Thus, while imagination, by itself, is not sufficient to lead to knowledge in Bachelard's view, in concert with the flexible rationalism of contemporary science, it can often be necessary in making such knowledge possible.

When it comes to the poetic image, imagination is, of course, both necessary and sufficient. For Bachelard finally to adopt the attitude of a "mere reader" whose reading may vary each time it is renewed,[1] is for him to recognize this singular feature of the poetic image. Moreover, he can do so without having to discard the underpinnings of a philosophy that permits flexibility in order to comment authentically on the object of its inquiry. As a reader, Bachelard allows the image to exist as an autonomous and irreducible symbolic reality. He no longer makes any attempt to discover its causes and he disregards its role within the totality of the work. Through his reading, he seeks to respond to the image as the independent product of an original consciousness. He finds receptive reading to be the best way to maintain the poet's creative reverie, the best means of keeping the poem alive, of truly communicating with the poet.

This posture seems a natural outgrowth of his repeated rejections of conceptual, positivistic methods of critical analysis throughout most of his work on the imagination. The specific nature of the image as the product of a creating consciousness requires a nonobjective method in order for it to be apprehended or "known," in the broadest sense of that term. But does rhis mean, as one critic has suggested, that there is "in Bachelard a settled prejudice in favor of reading and against criticism"?[2]

It is certainly true that Bachelard is a practitioner of careful reading as a means of responding to the literary image. It is equally true that he specifically rejects reductive critical approaches in order to read more faithfully. Nevertheless, he fully acknowledges the importance of conceptual criticism as a continuation of his own activity, particularly in the *Poetics*. As he explains in his introduction to *The Poetics of Space,* he deliberately chooses to "leave aside the problem of the *composition* of the poem as a grouping together of numerous images. Into this composition enter certain psychologically complex elements that associate earlier cultures with actual literary ideals—components which a complete phenomenology would no doubt be obliged to consider" (*PS,* xx–xxi). There is little doubt that a more "complete phenomenology," with its consideration of composition and cultural context, would be a more conceptual criticism than the willfully naive reading practiced by Bachelard. Akin to the in-*animus* reading mentioned in *The Poetics of Reverie,* it would serve to complement his own in-*anima* reading.

Thus, the fact that Bachelard himself chooses to become an in-*anima* reader does not mean that he no longer recognizes the necessity or even the possibility of a conceptual critical approach to literature. It merely means that, in order to respond adequately to the image, and ultimately to the poem, he must begin with an understanding of the image on its own terms and leave conceptual criticism to others. In the final analysis, what Bachelard opposes is not conceptual criticism, as such, but its substitution for an initial naive reading of the poem.[3] Where reason subsumes imagination in science, imagination must subsume reason in poetry.

The real question, then, is why, despite Bachelard's demonstrated ability to treat topics from a rigorously conceptual approach—one whose affinities with structuralism have been pointed out—he chooses a different means when it comes to literature. The answer is to be found in his recognition of the essential uniqueness of imaginative literature and, particularly, of its images. Such a recognition leads to an approach which Bachelard himself labelled "hermeneutic," as we have seen, an approach which is consistent with his fundamental position that philosophy must learn from the object of its analysis and with the related view that error stems from the imposition of a priori categories. These unaltered convictions growing out of his epistemology of science and applied to the literary image, are an important source of Bachelard's unity.

Because he was fully capable of speaking the conceptual language of criticism, including that of structuralism,[4] his warnings against a premature conceptualization of the work, which would destroy its imagistic meaning, are especially significant. Yet such admonitions can easily go unheeded when the work of some philosophers and critics most directly influenced by his epistemology is taken into account. Thus, French Marxist philosopher, Louis Althusser, although he separates himself from structuralism, implicitly recognizes the possibility of a broader application of Bachelard's epistemology when he derives the notion of "epistemological break" from Bachelard, while Michel Foucault, a former student of Althusser, makes a similar use of Bachelard's epistemology.[5] But their position does not lead, as does that of Bachelard to a recognition of the importance of an initially subjective approach to literature. With respect to Bachelard, at least, their view is a partial one, although it has the merit of recognizing Bachelard's epistemology as a potential source of critical commentary. The point is that any incomplete view of Bachelard, whether it concentrates on his oneiric or on his epistemological works, is likely to miss entirely a key feature of his contribution to literary criticism, namely that subjective and conceptual approaches need not be absolutely exclusive. As did Gérard Genette a few years after the *Poetics,* Bachelard, too, may be said to recognize the possibility that

the relation that unites structuralism and hermeneutics could be one, not of mechanical separation and exclusion, but of complementarity: with respect to the same work, hermeneutic criticism would speak the language of the recovery of meaning and of interior re-creation, and structural criticism the language of the distant word [*parole*] and of intelligible reconstruction. Thus they would draw complementary significances, and their dialogue would be all the more fruitful for it, except that both languages could never be spoken at once.[6]

Bachelard's most fundamental contribution to literary criticism is not to be found in any of several methods he may have used.[7] Nor is it to be deduced solely from his choice of hermeneutics over the more structural possibilities suggested by his epistemology of science. Rather, it is to be found in his refusal of orthodoxy, in his unwillingness absolutely to dismiss approaches, or "languages" other than his own, while insisting, in effect, that the individual critic avoid speaking "both languages at once." For Bachelard, the individual critic's commentary can never exhaust the possibilities of the work. It must, of necessity, be part of a colloquium of approaches which include methods that the individual critic himself might never apply. Bachelard's lesson is that criticism is a shared enterprise, a metalanguage made up of many voices, each with its own distinctive accent.

Notes and References

Chapter One

1. Reported by Pierre Thillet, one of Bachelard's former students at the Sorbonne, in "Table Ronde: Bachelard et l'enseignement," in *Bachelard: Colloque de Cerisy* (Paris, 1974), p. 423.

2. [Psychoanalysis of the Madman]. According to Jacques Gagey, who recounts this revealing misunderstanding in his *Gaston Bachelard ou la conversion à l'imaginaire* (Paris, 1969), p. 8n, the colleague in question had not yet read Bachelard's book.

3. Gaston Bachelard, "Castles in Spain," in *The Right to Dream,* trans. J. A. Underwood (New York, 1971), p. 86. In the same work, see also "Introduction to the Dynamics of Landscape," pp. 59–78, and "Albert Flocon's 'Engraver's Treatise,' " pp. 79–82.

4. François Dagognet, "Brunschvicg et Bachelard," *Revue de Métaphysique et de Morale* 70 (1965):43–54.

5. For an account of the "situation" of French literary criticism during Bachelard's lifetime, the reader should consult Laurent Le Sage, *The French New Criticism: An Introduction and a Sampler* (University Park and London: The Pennsylvania State University Press, 1967), pp. 3–22.

6. Following Bachelard's own practice, the term "poetry" will be used throughout this study to refer to literature in general. Bachelard has an obvious predilection for poetry, but he does not limit himself to that genre.

7. François Chatelet, "Gaston Bachelard, le prophète," *Arts-Loisirs* 843 (November 1961):15.

8. Albert Flocon, "Le Philosophe et le graveur," *Cerisy,* p. 274.

9. Gaston Bachelard, "Le Monde comme caprice et miniature" [The World as Caprice and Miniature], in *Études* [Studies], ed. Georges Canguilhem (Paris, 1970), pp. 25–43.

10. Georges Canguilhem, ed., preface to *L'Engagement rationaliste* [The Rationalist Commitment] (Paris, 1972), pp. 5–6. Dominique Lecourt, in his *Pour une critique de l'épistémologie (Bachelard, Canguilhem, Foucault)* (Paris, 1972), p. 14, sees a common ground among Bachelard, Canguilhem, and French historian of thought Michel Foucault in their

antievolutionary view of the history of science. To English-speaking readers this may suggest a correspondence between Bachelard and Thomas Kuhn's *The Structures of Scientific Revolutions* (Chicago: University of Chicago Press, 1962), but, in an introduction to the English edition of his work, entitled *Marxism and Epistemology; Bachelard, Canguilhem and Foucault,* trans. Ben Brewster (London, 1975), pp. 7–19, Lecourt insists that, despite surface similarities, there is a fundamental divergence between the "materialism" of Bachelard and the "idealism" of epistemologists like Kuhn. A rather different position is taken by Michel Vadée, who, in his *Bachelard ou le nouvel idéalisme épistémologique* (Paris, 1975), sees a fundamental idealism in Bachelard which can bring to a halt "the development of dialectical materialism" (287). Our purpose here is not to sort out the obvious ideological overtones of such questions, but merely to call attention to the continuing intellectual ferment which Bachelard's thought inspires.

11. For example, Georges Poulet, in "Bachelard et la conscience de soi," *Revue de Métaphysique et de Morale* 70 (1965):1–26, maintains that Bachelard is never simultaneously a scientist and a poet, and Jacques Gagey sees Bachelard's two directions as complementary (258), while Vincent Therrien speaks of the *"profound unity* of Bachelard's thought," in his *La Révolution de Gaston Bachelard en Critique Littéraire* (Paris, 1970), p. 66n, and Jean-Claude Margolin in his *Bachelard* (Paris, 1974), clearly "defends . . . the thesis of the unity of his thought" (10).

Chapter Two

1. Gaston Bachelard, *Essai sur la connaissance approchée* [An Essay on Knowledge by Approximation] (1928; rpt. Paris, 1973), p. 9. Hereafter cited as *ECA.*

2. Gaston Bachelard, *Étude sur l'évolution d'un problème de physique: La Propagation thermique dans les solides* [A Study on the Evolution of a Physics Problem: Heat Transfer in Solids] (1928, rpt. Paris, 1973). Hereafter cited as *EEPP.*

3. Georges Canguilhem, ed., Preface to *Études, p.* 7.

4. Gaston Bachelard, *L'Activité rationaliste de la physique contemporaine* [The Rationalist Activity of Contemporary Physics] (1951; rpt. Paris, 1977), p. 309. Hereafter cited as *ARPC.*

5. A position more amply developed by Roger Martin, "Épistémologie et philosophie," in *Hommage à Gaston Bachelard* (Paris, 1957), pp. 56–69.

6. Dominique Lecourt, *L'Épistémologie historique de Gaston Bachelard* (Paris, 1969), p. 42.

7. A. P. French, "Einstein—A condensed biography," in his *Einstein: A Centenary Volume* (Cambridge, Mass.: Harvard University Press, 1979), p. 57.

8. Gaston Bachelard, *La Valeur inductive de la relativité* [The Inductive Quality of Relativity] (Paris, 1929), p. 25. Hereafter cited as *VIR*.

9. Colin Smith, "The Role of Reason and the Concept as a Dissimilating Force," in his *Contemporary French Philosophy* (London: Methuen, 1964), pp. 108–14.

10. A[rthur] S[tanley] Eddington, *Space Time and Gravitation* (Cambridge: Cambridge University Press, 1923), p. 181.

11. Ibid., pp. 200–201.

12. A[rthur] S[tanley] Eddington, *The Mathematical Theory of Relativity,* 2nd ed. (Cambridge: Cambridge University Press, 1924), p. 41.

13. Gaston Bachelard, *Le Pluralisme cohérent de la chimie moderne* [The Coherent Pluralism of Modern Chemistry] (1932; rpt. Paris, 1973), p. 7. Hereafter cited as *PCCM*.

14. Georges Canguilhem, "L'Histoire des sciences dans l'oeuvre épistémologique de Gaston Bachelard," *Annales de l'Université de Paris* 33 (1963):24–39, has shown that Bachelard frequently uses a dialectical history of concepts in his epistemology. He attributes this approach to a predominance of rationalism over empiricism in Bachelard which requires that the past be judged according to contemporary scientific knowledge.

15. Throughout his epistemology, Bachelard frequently refers to the "prescientific" and "scientific" ages. While he normally does not claim a sharp temporal separation between the two and recognizes differences in the various sciences, the prescientific era is usually seen as ending with the eighteenth century, as is the case here. See also Chapter 3, p. 37.

Chapter Three

1. Gaston Bachelard, *Le Nouvel Esprit scientifique* [The New Scientific Mind] (1934; rpt. Paris, 1968), p. 3. Hereafter cited as *NES*.

2. For an account of the mathematics involved, addressed "to the liberal arts student and philosophy major as well as to the specialist in mathematics," p. xi, see David Gans, *An Introduction to Non-Euclidian Geometry* (New York: Academic Press, 1973).

3. Serge Doubrovsky has pointed out the relationship between the new scientific mind explored by Bachelard and structural linguistics in "La Crise de la critique française," *Nouvelle Revue Française* 214 (October 1970):65–66.

4. Jean Piaget, *Le Structuralisme* (Paris: Presses Universitaires de France, 1968), p. 6.

5. Ibid., p. 7.

6. In her "Ouverture et mobilité, parole et livre: un essai d'amour écrit,' " in *Cerisy,* pp. 246–58, Mary Ann Caws astutely observes that, for Bachelard, the encounter between science and poetry is not based on general principles which lead to immobility but on specific particulars which lead to openness and dynamism, and whose point of departure is "that of transcendence or *project*" (248).

7. For an additional discussion of creativity as a link between science and poetry, see E. Mary McAllester, "Unité de pensée chez Gaston Bachelard: Valeurs et langage," in *Cerisy,* pp. 91–110.

8. The proverb, "dis-moi qui tu fréquentes, je te dirai qui tu es" (Tell me with whom you associate, I will tell you who you are, or "Birds of a feather flock together") is frequently paraphrased by Bachelard, no doubt because it readily lends itself to comment about the nature of being.

9. Ann-Marie Denis, "Psychanalyse de la raison chez Gaston Bachelard," *Revue Philosophique de Louvain* 61 (1963):658.

10. Gaston Bachelard, *L'Expérience de l'espace dans la physique contemporaine* [The Experience of Space in Contemporary Physics] (Paris, 1937), p. 56. Hereafter cited as *EEPC.*

11. Gaston Bachelard, *La Formation de l'esprit scientifique: Contribution à une psychanalyse de la connaissance objective* [The Development of the Scientific Mind: A Contribution to a Psychology of Objective Knowledge] (Paris, 1938; rpt. Paris, 1972), p. 11. Hereafter cited as *FES.*

12. *FES,* 6–7. This discussion is somewhat more specific than earlier ones. See Chapter 2, note 15.

13. Gaston Bachelard, *The Philosophy of No: A Philsophy of the New Scientific Mind,* trans. G. C. Waterston (New York, 1968), p. 36. Hereafter cited as *PN.*

14. Gaston Bachelard, *Le Rationalisme appliqué* [Applied Rationalism] (1949; rpt. Paris, 1975), pp. 119–37.

15. Gaston Bachelard, *Le Matérialisme rationnel* [Rational Materialism] (1953; rpt. Paris, 1972), p. 223.

Chapter Four

1. Gagey, *Gaston Bachelard,* pp. 43–48.

2. Gaston Bachelard, *Les Intuitions atomistique (Essai de classification)* [Atomistic Intuitions (An Essay of Classification)] (1933; rpt. Paris, 1975), p. 12. Hereafter cited as *IA.*

3. Jean-Pierre Roy, in *Bachelard ou le concept contre l'image* (Montréal, 1977), pp. 17, 18, 46, et passim, argues that when the object of Bachelard's interest shifts from science to the imagination, there is a corresponding change in method from concept to image, although for Roy this transformation does not occur until *The Psychoanalysis of Fire* in 1938. Our position is that the transformation begins earlier and that it is not as extreme as Roy suggests until *The Poetics of Space* in 1957.

4. Gaston Bachelard, *L'Intuition de l'instant* [The Intuition of the Instant] (Paris, 1932), p. 5. Hereafter cited as *II.*

5. Gaston Roupnel, *Siloë* (Paris: Stock 1927).

6. Henri Bergson, "Essai sur les données immédiates de la conscience," in *Oeuvres* (Paris: Presses Universitaires de France, 1970), pp. 1–157. See also, "L'Évolution créatrice," in *Oeuvres,* p. 496 et passim. For a discussion of Bachelard's relationship to Bergson and others see Mary McAllester, "Polemics and Poetics: Bachelard's Conception of the Imagining Consciousness," *Journal of the British Society for Phenomenology* 12 (January 1981):3–13.

7. Bergson, *Oeuvres* p. 498.

8. Vadée, *Bachelard,* p. 124.

9. Ibid.

10. France Berçu, "Les Paradis perdus de Proust et de Bachelard," *L'Arc* 42 (1970):62–68, points out that Bachelard, like Proust, uses musical structures as metaphors when language inadequately conveys the reality of time. This is particularly so in *L'Intuition de l'instant* where Bachelard also makes several allusions to Proust, including a reference to a *"search for lost instants"* (*II,* 47).

11. Described by René de Costa, in *Vicente Huidobro y el creacionismo* (Madrid: Taurus, 1975), p. 13, as "simply one more name given to literary cubism," creationism is primarily a post–World War I, avant-garde, poetic phenomenon whose best-known exponent is not Pinheiro dos Santos but the Chilean poet Vicente Huidobro.

12. Gaston Bachelard, *La Dialectique de la durée* [The Dialectics of Duration] (1936; rpt. Paris, 1950), p. 142. Hereafter cited as *DD.*

13. Julien Naud, in *Structure et sens du symbole: L'Imaginaire chez Gaston Bachelard* (Tournai and Montréal, 1971), pp. 14, 202–3, et

passim, sees a similar opposition between vertical spiritual ascension and a material center in Bachelard's theory of the imagination. Although he confides that it "is not by the path of science that we wish to enter into Bachelard's work" (11), thereby limiting his investigation to Bachelard's theories of the imagination, our examination of the transitional *Dialectique de la durée* lends specific support to Naud's thesis and confirms his largely unexplored hunch that Bachelard's "studies on the imagination seem born of the continuation of the philosophy of science" (ibid.).

14. In *The Poetics of Space,* trans. Maria Jolas (New York, 1964), Bachelard berates the psychoanalyst because he "explains the flower by the fertilizer" (xxvi). Hereafter cited as *PS.*

15. Bachelard, "The Poetic Moment and the Metaphysical Moment," in *The Right to Dream,* p. 202.

16. Paul Valéry, *Le Cimetière Marin (The Graveyard by the Sea),* ed. and trans. Graham Dunstan Martin (Austin: University of Texas Press, 1971), p. 13.

17. Gaston Bachelard, "Le Surrationalisme" [Surrationalism], *Inquisitions* 1 (1936); rpt. in *L'Engagement rationaliste,* p. 12.

18. Valéry, *Le Cimetière,* p. 15.

Chapter Five

1. In an interview with Gilles G. Granger, *Paru,* January 1947, p. 56, Bachelard indicates, perhaps with tongue in cheek, that he wrote *The Psychoanalysis of Fire* in order to make use of a good bit of literary material left over from his background reading for *La Formation de l'esprit scientifique.*

2. *The Psychoanalysis of Fire,* trans. Alan C. M. Ross (Boston, 1964), p. 1. Hereafter cited as *PF.*

3. François Pire, in *De l'imagination poétique dans l'oeuvre de Gaston Bachelard* (Paris, 1967), p. 43, calls attention to Bachelard's independence with regard to Freud and to his affinities with Jung and other, more recent, psychologists.

4. First introduced in *La Dialectique de la durée,* where an "Orpheus complex" was associated with "a primitive need to please and to console" (*DD,* 148), it was then applied, as we have seen, to the realist's miserly attachment to substance as the "Harpagon complex" in *La Formation de l'esprit scientifique.*

5. In fact, the French, "les axes de la poésie et de la science sont d'abord inverses" (*La Psychanalyse du feu* [1938; rpt. Paris, 1949], p.

10) is more ambiguous than the English translation quoted earlier would indicate. Both context and semantics suggest the possibility that this sentence may actually mean that the axes of poetry and science are *initially* opposed.

6. Georges Poulet, in "Bachelard et la conscience de soi," finds that this closer identification of subject and object leads to increased self-awareness—a goal that had been unattainable in Bachelard's epistemology.

7. Gagey, *Gaston Bachelard*, p. 223.

8. In addition to the four elements, Bachelard muses on the possibility of a psychoanalysis of "salt, wine, and blood" (*PF,* 5), while Gilbert Durand, in "La Psychanalyse de la neige," *Mercure de France* 318 (1953):628, whimsically suggests that Bachelard's lowland background prevents him from considering the alpine element of snow.

9. Gaston Bachelard, *Lautréamont* (1939; rpt. Paris, 1951), p. 155. Hereafter cited as *L.*

10. Therrien, *La Révolution,* pp. 66n, 353. Despite his admirably thorough analysis of Bachelard's literary criticism and his proposition that there exists a fundamental link between the scientific and literary spirits in Bachelard, Therrien makes no sustained attempt to examine Bachelard's epistemology, as such. In our view it is important to analyze that epistemology directly, not only if we expect to demonstrate convincingly that such a link exists, but if we hope to understand how Bachelard's work on the literary imagination both continues and reacts to his epistemology.

11. Gaston Bachelard, *L'Eau et les rêves; Essai sur l'imagination de la matière* [Water and Dreams; An Essay on the Imagination of Matter] (Paris, 1942), p. 10. Hereafter cited as *ER.* See bibliography for an unpublished translation of this work.

12. According to Jean-Pierre Roy, *Bachelard,* (16–17), Bachelard's avowal of a rationalist goal in *L'Eau et les rêves* is merely an indication that his duality of method, corresponding to the duality of image and concept, requires constant effort. Yet Bachelard applies his struggle to become a rationalist not only to concepts but to "familiar images" (*ER,* 10); his purpose at this point is not to work at maintaining a duality of method, as Roy suggests, but to try to treat the disparate realms of knowledge and imagination rationally. While he admits an unreasoned fascination with water images, his rationalist *goal* does not change. It is, in fact, the underlying purpose of his entire taxonomy on the four elements.

13. Marie Bonaparte, *Edgar Poe* (Paris: Denoël et Steele, 1933).

14. Thus in Bachelard's "Introduction to Chagall's Bible," in *The Right to Dream*, "A single painting possesses inexhaustible eloquence. The colors become words" (9).

15. Edgar Allan Poe, *The Narrative of Arthur Gordon Pym*, in *Tales of Adventure and Exploration*, ed. Edmund Clarence Stedman and George Edward Woodberry (New York: Scribner, 1914), p. 301.

16. A term applied by Gilbert Durand, in "Science objective et conscience symbolique dans l'oeuvre de Gaston Bachelard," *Cahiers du Sud* 4 (1964):48.

17. Mary Ann Caws, *Surrealism and the Literary Imagination: A Study of Breton and Bachelard* (The Hague, 1966), p. 16.

18. In his *Gaston Bachelard et les éléments* (Paris, 1967), pp. 146–80, undoubtedly the most extensive analysis of the *Elements*, Michel Mansuy explores Bachelard's pioneering work in this area and identifies several "laws" of the imagination, although Bachelard himself is never very systematic in codifying such laws. See also Mansuy's "Gaston Bachelard et les lois de l'imagination littéraire," *Travaux de Linguistique et de Littérature* 4 (1966):103–109, for a similar discussion.

Chapter Six

1. Lithuanian-born Oscar Vladislas de Lubicz-Milosz, known as O. V. de L. Milosz, was reared and educated in France, where he wrote poetry during the first third of the twentieth century. He is the great-uncle of Czeslaw Milosz, winner of the 1980 Nobel prize for literature.

2. Gaston Bachelard, *L'Air et les songes; Essai sur l'imagination du mouvement* [Air and Dreams; An Essay on the Imagination of Motion] (Paris, 1943), p. 10. Hereafter cited as *AS*.

3. Jean-Louis Backès, "Sur le mot continuité," *L'Arc* 42 (1970):69–75, calls attention to the fact that, in both science and poetry, Bachelard rejects the notion of continuity when it is immobile but that he sees it in a favorable light when, as is the case here, it is dynamic.

4. Bachelard frequently has been criticized for attributing to every writer what Georges Poulet calls the same "coefficient of genius" ("Kritiker von heute," *Schweizer Monatshefte* 44 [1964]:360). The criticism is undoubtedly deserved and should give pause to those inclined to view Bachelard primarily as a practicing literary critic.

5. Suzanne Hélein-Koss calls attention to the problem of the ingenuous application of Bachelard's theories in her "Gaston Bachelard:

Vers une nouvelle méthodologie de l'image littéraire?" *French Review* 45 (1971):362–64.

6. In the concluding chapter of *La Terre et les rêveries de la volonté,* Bachelard will return to Desoille's theory when he considers anew dreams of ascent and descent in the context of the terrestrial imagination.

7. Sigmund Freud, "Formulations on the Two Principles of Mental Functioning," in *The Standard Edition of the Complete Psychological Works of Sigmund Freud,* trans. and ed. James Strachey (London: Hogarth Press, 1958), 12: 218–19.

8. E[ugène] Minkowski in "Vers quels horizons nous emmène Gaston Bachelard?" *Revue Internationale de Philosophie* 17 (1973):424, sees in Bachelard's attempt to "repoeticize life" in *L'Air et les songes,* a response to the denudation brought about by discursive thought.

9. Gaston Bachelard, *La Terre et les rêveries de la volonté: Essai sur l'imagination des forces* [Earth and Reveries of Will: An Essay on the Imagination of Forces] (Paris, 1948), p. 10. Hereafter cited as *TRV.* See the bibliography for an unpublished translation of this work.

10. The reader interested in exploring further the relationship between Bachelard and Sartre should consult François Pire, *De l'imagination,* for whom dynamism is the primary element of Bachelard's poetic imagination (93), and who undertakes a careful comparison of Sartre's theories in *L'Imagination* (1936) and *L'Imaginaire* (1940) with Bachelard's view on the imagination (152–66). For a similar discussion, see also Ronald Grimsley, "Two Philosophical Views of the Literary Imagination: Sartre and Bachelard," *Comparative Literature Studies* 8 (1971):42–57.

11. For further discussion of Bachelard's comments on *La Nausée,* see Mechthild Cranston, *"Ding* and *Werk:* Heidegger and the Dialectics of Bachelard's *Image," Rivista di Letterature Moderne e Comparate* 32 (June 1979):1302–37.

12. For a detailed and inspired account of the kinship between Bachelard and the surrealists, particularly André Breton, the reader should consult Mary Ann Caws's imaginative study on Breton and Bachelard.

13. Gaston Bachelard, *La Terre et les rêveries du repos: Essai sur les images de l'intimité* [Earth and Reveries of Repose: An Essay on Images of Intimacy] (Paris, 1948), p. 320. Hereafter cited as *TRR.*

14. Jean-Paul Sartre, *What Is Literature?* trans. Bernard Frechtman (New York: Harper & Row, 1965), p. 12.

15. Writing on "Gaston Bachelard" in *Modern French Criticism: From Proust and Valéry to Structuralism,* ed. John K. Simon (Chicago: Uni-

versity of Chicago Press, 1972), Robert Champigny calls Bachelard's increasing interest in language used aesthetically a "conversion to quality" (184).

16. More recently J. Hillis Miller has reached a similar conclusion in his "Ariadne's Thread: Repetition and the Narrative Line," *Critical Inquiry* 3 (1976), where, with a metaphor worthy of Bachelard, he points out that "the chase has a beast in view. The end of the story is the retrospective revelation of the law of the whole" (69).

Chapter Seven

1. Such empirical reduction to "external" causes of the phenomenon should not be confused with phenomenological reduction, a process by which the phenomenon, defined in its special relationship of consciousness and reality, is reduced to its own "internal" essence.

2. According to the editor of *The Poetics of Space*, "Eugene Minkowski, a prominent phenomenologist whose studies extend both in the fields of psychology and philosophy, followed Bergson in accepting the notion of 'élan vital' as the dynamic origin of human life" (*PS*, xiin). Bachelard's previous analysis of time, however, in which he attacked Bergson's notion of duration, argues against assuming that he borrowed anything more than the term from Minkowski. Reverberation (*retentissement*) acquires a meaning that fits Bachelard's own phenomenology in *The Poetics of Space*.

3. Gabriel Germain, "L'Imagination poétique et la notion de métapsychologie chez Bachelard," in *Cerisy*, pp. 182–95. See especially pp. 190–91.

4. Gaston Bachelard, *The Poetics of Reverie*, trans. Daniel Russell (New York, 1969), p. 209. Hereafter cited as *PR*.

5. Jean-Pierre Roy sees a "refusal of science" (7) in Bachelard's adoption of a nonconceptual method when dealing with the image. Left unresolved, given Bachelard's obvious familiarity with science, is the significance of his methodological choice for literary criticism. This issue will be addressed in our conclusion.

6. Early twentieth-century technology literally gives the planet a voice through radio. In "Reverie and Radio," first published in *La Nef* in 1951 and later included in the posthumous *Right to Dream* (188–94), Bachelard explores the essential role of reverie within the "logosphere" of radio.

7. For Pascal the separation between finesse and geometry is related to the distinction between everyday perception and science: "For it is

to judgement that perception belongs, as science belongs to the intellect. Subtlety [*finesse*] is the business of judgement, geometry of intellect" (Blaise Pascal, *Pensées,* ed. Louis Lafuma, trans. John Warrington [London: J. M. Dent and Sons, 1960], p. 266).

8. See Chapter 3, p. 29.

9. Gaston Bachelard, *La Flamme d'une chandelle* [The Candleflame] (Paris, 1961), p. 1. Hereafter cited as *FC.*

10. In his "Du calcul des improbabilités," *Cahiers Internationaux du Symbolisme* 6 (1964):69–87, Bachelard's longtime friend the poet Jean Lescure made passing reference to the manuscript of *La Poétique du Phénix,* of which he has custody. He later provided excerpts from the introduction of this work to Jean-Claude Margolin, who included them in his study on Bachelard (97–98).

Chapter Eight

1. In *La Flamme d'une chandelle,* Bachelard acknowledges that "never have I read in the same way twice. . . . What a poor professor of literature I would have made!" (105).

2. Roy, *Bachelard,* p. 175.

3. E. Mary McAllester makes a similar observation in "Gaston Bachelard: Towards a Phenomenology of Literature," *Forum for Modern Language Studies* 12 (April 1976):96. Her related and fundamental view that Bachelard's epistemology leads to his phenomenology is quite perceptive, although we would take exception to her arguments purporting to show the directness of such a link based on her reduction of Bachelard's epistemology primarily to portions of *La Connaissance approchée.*

4. A possibility Ricardou could not, or would not, foresee when he attacked Bachelard's hermeneutics in "Le Caractère singulier de cette eau," *Critique* 23 (1967):718–33. See also Tom and Verena Conley's comment on Ricardou's observations, in their "Ideological Warfare: Ricardou's Purge of Bachelard," *Sub-Stance* 1 (1971):71–78.

5. In "A Letter to the Translator," in his and Etienne Balibar's *Reading Capital,* 2nd ed. (London: NLB, 1977), Althusser points out that while "This term [epistemological break] is rarely to be found as such in Bachelard's texts . . . the *thing* is there all the time from a certain point on in Bachelard's work. . . . As for Foucault, the uses he explicitly or implicitly makes of the concepts of 'break' . . . are echoes either of Bachelard, or of my own systematic 'use' of Bachelard" (323). The term is related to what we have called Bachelard's "transcendent science."

6. Gérard Genette, *Figures* (Paris: Editions du Seuil, 1966), p. 161.

7. Vincent Therrien identifies eight such methods which, however, "are strongly unified in a 'coherent pluralism' " (344; see also pp. 195–342).

Selected Bibliography

PRIMARY SOURCES

Place of publication is Paris unless otherwise noted. Dates following the title and publisher are those of the first French edition. Dates and editions in parentheses indicate more recent editions used in this study. For a sequential list of Bachelard's works see Chronology.

1. Major Publications

L'Activité rationaliste de la physique contemporaine. Presses Universitaires de France, 1951 (Union Générale d'Editions, 1977).

L'Air et les songes: Essai sur l'imagination du mouvement. Corti, 1943.

La Dialectique de la durée. Boivin, 1936 (Presses Universitaires de France, Nouvelle édition, 1950).

L'Eau et les rêves: Essai sur l'imagination de la matière. Corti, 1942.

Essai sur la connaissance approchée. Vrin, 1928 (4th ed., 1973).

Étude sur l'évolution d'un problème de physique: La propagation thermique dans les solides. Vrin, 1928 (2nd ed., 1973).

L'Expérience de l'espace dans la physique contemporaine. Alcan, 1937.

La Flamme d'une chandelle. Presses Universitaires de France, 1961.

La Formation de l'esprit scientifique: Contribution à une psychanalyse de la connaissance objective. Vrin, 1938 (8th ed., 1972).

L'Intuition de l'instant. Stock, 1932 (Gonthier, 1932).

Les Intuitions atomistiques (Essai de classification). Boivin, 1933 (Vrin, 2nd ed., 1975).

Lautréamont. Corti, 1939 (Nouvelle édition augmentée, 1951).

Le Matérialisme rationnel. Presses Universitaires de France, 1953 (3d ed., 1972).

Le Nouvel Esprit scientifique. Alcan, 1934 (Presses Universitaires de France, 10th ed., 1968).

La Philosophie du non: Essai d'une philosophie du nouvel esprit scientifique. Presses Universitaires de France, 1940.

Le Pluralisme cohérent de la chimie moderne. Vrin, 1932 (2nd ed., 1973).

La Poétique de la rêverie. Presses Universitaires de France, 1960.
La Poétique de l'espace. Presses Universitaires de France, 1957.
La Psychanalyse du feu. Gallimard, 1938 (Collection Idées, 1949).
Le Rationalisme appliqué. Presses Universitaires de France, 1949 (5th ed., 1975).
La Terre et les rêveries de la volonté: Essai sur l'imagination des forces. Corti, 1948.
La Terre et les rêveries du repos: Essai sur les images de l'intimité. Corti, 1948.
La Valeur inductive de la relativité. Vrin, 1929.

2. Editions
These make available Bachelard's most important minor works.
Le Droit de rêver. Presses Universitaires de France, 1970. Collection of previously published essays on art, literature, and reverie.
L'Engagement rationaliste. Edited by Georges Canguilhem. Presses Universitaires de France, 1972. Collection of lectures and previously published articles on the epistemology of science.
Épistémologie. Edited by Dominique Lecourt. Presses Universitaires de France, 1971. Excerpts from Bachelard's epistemological works.
Études. Edited by Georges Canguilhem. Presses Universitaires de France, 1970. Collection of previously published essays written between 1931 and 1934.

3. English Translations
On Poetic Imagination and Reverie. Translated and edited by Colette Gaudin. Indianapolis: Bobbs-Merrill, 1971. Selections from works on the imagination, with an introduction by the translator.
"The Philosophic Dialectic of the Concepts of Relativity." Translated by Forrest W. Williams. In *Albert Einstein: Philosopher—Scientist.* Edited by Paul Arthur Schilpp. Evanston, Ill.: Library of Living Philosophers, 1949, pp. 563–80. The French Version, "La Dialectique philosophique des notions de la relativité," does not appear until 1972, in *L'Engagement rationaliste,* pp. 120–36.
The Philosophy of No; A Philosophy of the New Scientific Mind. Translated by G. C. Waterston. New York: Orion Press, 1969.
The Poetics of Reverie. Translated by Daniel Russell. New York: Orion Press, 1969; under the title *The Poetics of Reverie; Childhood, Language and the Cosmos.* Boston: Beacon Press, 1971.
The Poetics of Space. Translated by Maria Jolas. New York: Orion Press, 1964; Boston: Beacon Press, 1969.

The Psychoanalysis of Fire. Translated by Alan C. M. Ross. Boston: Beacon Press, 1964; London: Routledge and Kegan Paul, 1964.

The Right to Dream. Translated by J. A. Underwood. New York: Grossman, 1971.

Two of Bachelard's works have been translated as part of American doctoral dissertations: Edith Rodgers Farrell, *"Water and Dreams by Gaston Bachelard: An Annotated Translation with Introduction by the Translator,"* Diss. State University of Iowa, 1965; and Liliana Zancu, "Transcendental Dynamics: A Bachelardian Romantic Perspective Including the English Translation of *Earth and Reveries of Volition: An Essay on the Imagination of Forces* by Gaston Bachelard," Diss. Kent State University, 1975.

SECONDARY SOURCES

Given the number of critical commentaries on Bachelard's work, many worthy contributions could not be included in this highly selective list. Several are mentioned in the notes. Additional references may be found in Jean Rummens, "Gaston Bachelard: une bibliographie," *Revue Internationale de Philosophie* 17 (1963):492–504, and in several books on Bachelard listed below, most notably in the studies of Jacques Gagey, Jean-Claude Margolin, Jean-Pierre Roy, and Vincent Therrien. The reader interested in a more detailed critical commentary than the confines of this study will allow should consult our "Gaston Bachelard," in *A Critical Bibliography of French Literature,* edited by Douglas W. Alden and Richard B. Brooks (Syracuse: Syracuse University Press, 1980), VI, Part 3, 1423–31.

1. Books

Caws, Mary Ann. *Surrealism and the Literary Imagination: A Study of Breton and Bachelard.* The Hague: Mouton, 1966. An imaginative comparison of each writer's poetic theories, although the treatment of Bachelard is somewhat uneven.

Dagognet, François. *Gaston Bachelard, sa vie, son oeuvre, avec un exposé de sa philosophie.* Paris: Presses Universitaires de France, 1965. A concise introduction to Bachelard, including excerpts from his works.

Dionigi, Roberto. *Gaston Bachelard. La "filosofia" come ostaculo episte-mologico.* Padua: Marsilio, 1973. Reviews the main themes of Bachelard's epistemology.

Gagey, Jacques. *Gaston Bachelard ou la conversion à l'imaginaire.* Paris: Marcel Rivière, 1969. A penetrating inquiry into the philosophical and cultural implications of Bachelard's transition to the works on the imagination.

Ginestier, Paul. *La Pensée de Bachelard.* Paris: Bordas, 1968. A sympathetic but sketchy and excessively rigid examination of Bachelard's ideas in both science and art.

Lalonde, Maurice. *La Théorie de la connaissance scientifique selon Gaston Bachelard.* Montréal: Fides, 1966. A systematic, though doctrinaire presentation of Bachelard's epistemology from a neoscholastic perspective.

Lecourt, Dominique. *Bachelard: Le Jour et la nuit.* Paris: Grasset, 1974. A closely argued analysis, based on Marxist premises, of what the author considers to be Bachelard's failed attempt to escape from philosophical presuppositions with respect to science.

————. *L'Epistémologie historique de Gaston Bachelard.* Paris: Vrin, 1969. A Marxist reading of Bachelard's epistemology which credits him with abandoning philosophical idealism.

————. *Marxism and Epistemology; Bachelard, Canguilhem and Foucault.* Translated by Ben Brewster. London: NLB, 1975. Combines his 1969 book and his 1974 book below into one volume with an introduction directed to English-speaking audiences.

————. *Pour une critique de l'épistémologie (Bachelard, Canguilhem, Foucault).* Paris: Maspero, 1974. Attempts to establish a link between the three philosophers based on their rejection of both a positivistic epistemology and an evolutionary view of the history of science.

Mansuy, Michel. *Gaston Bachelard et les éléments.* Paris: Corti, 1967. A thorough and readable appraisal of the *Elements*.

Margolin, Jean-Claude. *Bachelard.* Paris: Seuil, 1974. A concise and attractively illustrated introduction to Bachelard, including selections from his works.

Messina, Daniela. *Bachelard: I segmenti della ragione.* Bologna: Zanielli, 1977. An introduction to Bachelard's epistemology accompanied by selections.

Naud, Julien. *Structure et sens du symbole; L'Imaginaire chez Gaston Bachelard.* Tournai: Desclée; Montréal: Bellarmin, 1971. Explains the imaginary in Bachelard as a dynamic tension between matter and spirit which points to a transcendent reality.

Pire, François. *De l'imagination poétique dans l'oeuvre de Gaston Bachelard.* Paris: Corti, 1967. Thorough discussion of the works on the imagination, including many interesting comparisons of Bachelard to other writers and an excellent analysis of his phenomenology.

Préclaire, Madeleine. *Une Poétique de l'homme; Essai sur l'imagination d'après l'oeuvre de Gaston Bachelard.* Tournai: Desclée; Montréal: Bellarmin, 1971. Considers the ethical implications of Bachelard's theory of the imagaination.

Quillet, Pierre. *Bachelard.* Paris: Seghers, 1964. An informed analysis of Bachelard's thought within the intellectual context of his time, followed by selections from his works.

Robertz, Egon. *Feur und Traum. Studien zur Literaturkritik Gaston Bachelards.* Frankfurt: Lang, 1978. A methodical exploration of Bachelard's works on the imagination which stresses his contribution to an undogmatic method of receptive reading.

Roy, Jean-Pierre. *Bachelard ou le concept contre l'image.* Montréal: Les Presses Universitaires de Montréal, 1977. A closely reasoned and well-documented analysis which argues that Bachelard's work is flawed by his abandonment of conceptual methods when dealing with the image.

Schaettel, Marcel. *Bachelard critique ou l'alchimie du rêve; Un Art de lire et de rêver.* Lyon: L'Hermès, 1977. An undogmatic attempt to explore, classify, and extend Bachelard's notions on reading.

Sertoli, Guiseppe. *Le immagini e la realtà; Saggio su Gaston Bachelard.* Florence: La Nuova Italia, 1972. Argues that Bachelard sought a surreality beyond the impurity of reality, in both science and poetry.

Therrien, Vincent. *La Révolution de Gaston Bachelard en critique littéraire; Ses Fondements, ses techniques, sa portée: Du nouvel esprit scientifique à un nouvel esprit littéraire.* Paris: Klincksieck, 1970. A meticulous, original, and well-documented analysis of Bachelard's commentary on literature, with particular focus on *Lautréamont* and the lesser-known articles and prefaces.

Vadée, Michel. *Bachelard ou le nouvel idéalisme épistémologique.* Paris: Editions Sociales, 1975. A thorough, critical analysis of Bachelard's thought for the purpose of purging French Marxism and structuralism of its influence.

Voisin, Marcel. *Bachelard.* Brussels: Labor, 1967. General introduction, including excerpts and a glossary of Bachelard's terms.

2. Collected Articles

L'Arc 42 (1970):1–90. "Bachelard." Whole issue devoted to Bachelard, with important and occasionally highly original articles by Jean-Louis Backès, France Berçu, Michel-G. Bernard, Raymond Jean, Gilbert Lascault, Dominique Lecourt, Jean-F. Lyotard, Michel Serres, and Hélène Védrine.

Bachelard: Colloque de Cerisy. Paris: Union Générale d'Editions, 1974. Papers and discussion from the 1970 Colloquium on Bachelard at Cerisy-la-Salle. Many useful and informative articles including contributions by Mary Ann Caws, Jean Follain, Marie-Louise Gouhier, Michel Guiomar, Jean Lescure, E. Mary McAllester, Jacques Plessen, René Poirier, Clémence Ramnoux, Marcel Schaettel, and others.

Cahiers du sud 51 (1964):179–206. "Gaston Bachelard et les poètes." Special section of this issue on Bachelard with articles of varying quality by Jean-Pierre Faye, Pierre Gardère, Louis Guillaume, and Max Picard.

Critique 20 (1964):3–51. "Gaston Bachelard (1884–1962)." Special section of this issue on Bachelard with articles by Jean Catesson, Maurice-Jean Lefebvre, and Jean-Claude Pariente.

Hommage à Gaston Bachelard: Etudes de philosophie et d'histoire des sciences. Paris: Presses Universitaires de France, 1957. Articles by Georges Canguilhem and Roger Martin on Bachelard's epistemology, and by Jean Hyppolite on science and the imagination.

Nuova Corrente 64 (1974):201–365. "Bachelard e la scienza." Special section of this issue on Bachelard which attempts to broaden the discussion of Bachelard's epistemology beyond recent Marxist interpretations. Includes contributions by Francesco Barone, Alma Maria Comis, Vittorio Cotesta, Francesco Fistetti, Gilles-Gaston Granger, and Marcello Pera.

Revue Internationale de Philosophie 17 (1963):419–529. Special issue on Bachelard with articles on his epistemology and his theory of the imagination, including contributions by Francesco Barone, Georges Canguilhem, C. G. Christofides, E. Minkowski, and Jean Rummens.

3. Articles and Chapters

Blanchot, Maurice. "Vaste comme la nuit." *Nouvelle Revue Française* 7 (1959):684–95; also in his *L'Entretien infini.* Paris: Gallimard, 1969, pp. 465–77. Like the word "vaste" in Baudelaire, Bachelard's image is seen as a possibility rather than a representation.

Canguilhem, Georges. "L'Histoire des sciences dans l'oeuvre épistémologique de Gaston Bachelard." *Annales de l'Université de Paris* 33 (1963):24–39. A perceptive article on the alliance of epistemology and the history of science in Bachelard.

Champigny, Robert. "Gaston Bachelard." In *Modern French Criticism: From Proust and Valéry to Structuralism.* Edited by John K. Simon. Chicago: University of Chicago Press, 1972, pp. 175–91. A first-rate and nuanced examination of Bachelard's contribution to literary criticism.

Christofides, C. G. "Gaston Bachelard's Phenomenology of the Imagination." *Romanic Review* 52 (1961):36–47. Excerpts from a 1957 interview with Bachelard make this analysis of Bachelard's psychoanalytic dimension particularly useful.

Cranston, Mechthild. *"Ding* and *Werk*: Heidegger and the Dialectics of Bachelard's *Image."* *Rivista di Letterature Moderne e Comparate* 32 (June 1979):130–37. Discussion of Bachelard's dynamic imagery within the context of Heidegger's thought.

Diéguez, Manual De. "Gaston Bachelard." In his *L'Écrivain et son langage.* Paris: Gallimard, 1960, pp. 221–33. Claims that Bachelard sees poetry as a means of knowledge but that he clings to the primacy of reason.

Ehrmann, Jacques. "Introduction to Gaston Bachelard." *Modern Language Notes* 8 (1966):572–78. Credits Bachelard with renewing French literary criticism despite the shortcomings of his subjective and fragmentary approach.

Elevitch, Bernard. "Gaston Bachelard: The Philosopher as Dreamer." *Dialogue: Canadian Philosophical Review* 7 (1968–69):430–48. A closely argued analysis, which finds Bachelard's greatest strength in his criticism rather than in his philosophy.

Gaudin, Colette. "L'Imagination et la rêverie: Remarques sur la poétique de Gaston Bachelard." *Symposium* 20 (1966):207–25. Very thorough, though somewhat inconclusive, discussion of Bachelard's writing on literature.

Gouhier, Marie-Louise. "Bachelard et le surréalisme." In *Entretiens sur le surréalisme.* Edited by Ferdinand Alquié. The Hague: Mouton, 1968. Claims that, like the surrealists, Bachelard sees poetry as liberation but that he does not seek a union of life and poetry.

Grimsely, Ronald. "Two Philosophical Views of the Literary Imagination: Sartre and Bachelard." *Comparative Literature Studies* 8 (1971):42–57. Emphasizes the similarities between Sartre's and

Bachelard's views of the imagination as a prereflective conscious activity.

Hans, James S. "Gaston Bachelard and the Phenomenology of the Reading Consciousness." *Journal of Aesthetics and Art Criticism* 35 (1977):315–27. An analysis of the *Poetics* which concludes that Bachelard's phenomenology leads to a fragmented view of the poem.

Hélein-Koss, Suzanne. "Gaston Bachelard: Vers une nouvelle méthodologie de l'image littéraire?" *French Review* 45 (1971):353–64. Bachelard's contribution to critical methodology is assessed, with the conclusion that he is more of a philosopher of the imagination than a theoretician of literature.

Heusch, Luc De. "Anthropologie structurale et symbolisme." *Cahier Internationaux de Symbolisme* 2 (1963):51–65. Sees the semantic function of myth as a means of linking structural anthropology and the *Elements*.

Jones, Robert Emmet. "Gaston Bachelard." In his *Panorama de la nouvelle critique en France*. Paris: SEDES, 1968, pp. 39–76. Sees in Bachelard an arbitrary, subjective, and pseudoscientific precursor of French new criticism.

Kushner, Eva M. "The Critical Method of Gaston Bachelard." In *Myth and Symbol. Critical Approaches and Applications*. Edited by Bernice Slote. Lincoln: University of Nebraska Press, 1963, pp. 39–50. Sees a test for the authenticity of images as central to Bachelard's method.

Martin, Roger. "Dialectique et esprit scientifique chez Gaston Bachelard." *Études Philosophiques* 18 (1963):409–19. Claims that Bachelard uses a Hegelian dialectic to overcome a contradiction between rationalism and empiricism in his epistemology.

McAllester, E. Mary. "Gaston Bachelard: Towards a Phenomenology of Literature." *Forum for Modern Language Studies* 12 (April 1976):91–104. Argues perceptively that it is the value of creativity in Bachelard's epistemology which allows him to initiate a phenomenology of literature.

———. "Polemics and Poetics: Bachelard's Conception of the Imagining Consciousness." *Journal of the British Society for Phenomenology* 12 (January 1981):3–13. Lucidly maintains that Bachelard's work on science and poetry is united by his conception of human consciousness as polemical and creative.

Poulet, Georges. "Bachelard et la conscience de soi." *Revue de Métaphysique et de Morale* 70 (1965):1–26; also "Gaston Bachelard," parts II–VI, in his *La Conscience critique*. Paris: Corti, 1971, pp. 175–208. Bachelard's phenomenology is seen as a valid method of literary criticism in this subtle exploration of the subject-object relationship in his thought.

————. "Bachelard et la critique contemporaine." In *Currents of Thought in French Literature. Essays in Memory of G. T. Clapton.* New York: Barnes and Noble, 1966, pp. 353–57. Points to Bachelard's idea of the materiality of consciousness as a revolutionary contribution to literary criticism.

Ricardou, Jean. "Le Caractère singulier de cette eau." *Critique* 243–44 (1967):718–33; also in his *Problèmes du nouveau roman.* Paris: Seuil, 1967, pp. 193–207. Uses Bachelard's interpretation of Poe in *L'Eau et les rêves* to illustrate a challenge to hermeneutics.

Smith, Roch C. "Gaston Bachelard and Critical Discourse: The Philosopher of Science as Reader." *Stanford French Review* 5 (Fall 1981):217–28. Suggests that Bachelard's emphasis on reading is consistent with his philosophical concerns and with the goal of a flexible literary criticism.

————. "Gaston Bachelard and the Power of Poetic Being." *French Literature Series* 4 (1977):235–38. Sees the moment of creation as a link between science and poetry in Bachelard.

Solomon, Jacques. "M. Gaston Bachelard et le 'nouvel esprit scientifique.' " *La Pensée: Revue du Rationalisme Moderne* (nouvelle série) 2 (1945):47–55. An early challenge to Bachelard's views on the relationship of scientific theory to reality.

Souriau, Etienne. "L'Esthétique de Gaston Bachelard." *Annales de l'Université de Paris* 33 (1963):11–23. Argues that Bachelard's epistemology has an aesthetic dimension while the works on the imagination seek knowledge of self and man, with creative reverie as the unifying element.

Tuzet, Hélène. "Les Voies ouvertes par Gaston Bachelard à la critique littéraire." In *Les Chemins actuels de la critique.* Edited by Georges Poulet. Paris: Plon, 1967, pp. 359–71; another ed., Paris: Union Générale d'Editions, 1968, pp. 201–13. Claims that, despite Bachelard's disavowal of a goal of criticism, his works on the imagination suggest many possibilities to the literary critic.

Index